Long Live Southbank

Long Live Southbank

Contents

Introduction

In March 2013, the Southbank Centre in London unveiled plans for the 'Festival Wing', a £120 million redevelopment scheme that would see the iconic skateboarding, BMXing and street arts space underneath the Queen Elizabeth Hall transformed into retail units. As a reaction to this news, Long Live Southbank was born and the idea for this book conceived.

To millions of people around the world, the area now known as the 'Undercroft' is a treasured space, known as the birthplace of British skateboarding and home to skateboarders, BMX riders and graffiti artists for the last 40 years. Southbank is the oldest recognised and still existing skateboarding space in the world and is a living, breathing testimony to the power of creativity, community and organic public space.

Despite the thousands of magazine articles, hours of video footage and photographs documenting the daily happenings of this vibrant spot on London's Southbank, to date nobody has produced a definitive history of this iconic space. Seeing our beloved spot under threat we felt it was time to bring together the hundreds of unique voices and their experiences, to tell the stories of the late nights and early mornings spent riding the banks, to remember the trials and tribulations of the different crews who have frequented the underbelly of these Brutalist buildings throughout all seasons and conditions. We felt it was time to commit their history to physical memory, in their own words, through their own eyes, in order to learning new crafts and testing their physical limits, often while rubbing shoulders with the same faces they've seen in magazines and on television.

Southbank is not just a skate spot. It is not just a place where people go to practice. Southbank is a community of creatives who have pushed the boundaries of their craft and developed a hub of diversity, skill and ingenuity. While the location was built with no particular purpose in mind, and left unused, they brought life, imagination and vitality to its concrete slabs, seeing challenges to be overcome where others saw a desolate urban no man's land.

Our campaign, Long Live Southbank, is dedicated to protecting the Undercroft, as it is in its current form. We encourage this because we believe its cultural and historical status to be irreplaceable and that its unique architecture and the vitality of its thriving community should be present for future generations.

Long Live Southbank is committed to the protection of the Undercroft that has given birth to a rare artistic creativity and community, which continues to flourish. This book is about that journey and serves as a reminder of what a community can achieve when it has a vision.

Long Live Southbank

Croydan and Roger Gonzales

Ben Jobe

David Yap

Arun Grogna, Craig Jackson and Finn Andres

Mark Gonzalez
Hippy Jump

The Home of British Skateboarding

Ben Powell

Every cultural movement with global significance has its own spiritual home; that place where things begin, which then acts as the catalyst for everything that follows. The Blues has the Deep South, Detroit Techno has Belleville, Michigan, Punk has CBGBs and the King's Road in London, Cubism had the Salle 41 in Paris, 60s counter culture had the Haight-Ashbury district of San Francisco and so on and so forth. The Southbank is UK skateboarding's spiritual home.

Long before the original skateboard boom of the mid 1970s gave birth to custom-built and monetized skateboard-specific facilities such as the now monolithic skate parks of Harrow, Romford, Meanwhile and Royal Oak, the Southbank was the universally-celebrated home of skateboarding in the UK.

It was never designed for this purpose, nor did the designers of the space ever imagine this eventuality, but less than a decade after its construction, skateboarders found it and infused it with meaning.

Prior to being given life by skateboarding, the area referred to as the Undercroft had no intrinsic value, other than to direct pedestrian traffic from one side of the building to the other. It was literally a void, a space beneath a space – gloomy, occasionally dangerous, and devoid of purpose until its bounties were discovered, exploited and enjoyed by the nascent skateboarding scene of the early 1970s.

This is not to say that the Southbank is alone in occupying this cultural position – far from it – but, crucially, it is one of only a scant few such spaces that still remain.

The Justin Herman Plaza in San Francisco, (more commonly known as 'EMB'), Love Park in Philadelphia, the Brooklyn Banks in New York, Central TV in Birmingham, Old Market Square in Nottingham and many more all played a similar role in nurturing and contributing to a global culture shared through magazines and videos, but eventually all of these spaces were demolished, redeveloped or similarly extinguished.

The Southbank Undercroft, even in its current state where a good 70% of the original space is gone, is the oldest, still-extant city skate spot in the entire world. It has been a central, iconic and continuous anchor of both UK and global skateboarding culture for nearly five decades.

Over that time, this simple paved space has generated hundreds of thousands of photographs, countless hours of video footage, life-long friendships, careers, relationships and everything besides that you would associate with a genuine and constantly evolving community.

It is real, living heritage – accessible, for free, to anybody, (regardless of age, ethnicity, gender or any other subdivision of life) who wants to join in the fun.

The Undercroft has culture, tradition and joy ingrained into the very materials from which it was created and we, as skateboarders, not any outside authority, made it that way.

It's not necessary for you to have the slightest knowledge about the intricacies or history of skateboarding culture to understand that the above is fact: all you need to do is take a walk along the Thames and see for yourself.

The Undercroft is alive and the echoes of its past and present meaning to millions of people are in plain sight for anybody who takes the time to venture down there and watch the daily life of the place.

History, tradition, heritage and community are precious things, which cannot just be relocated. This is your city, just as much as it is ours, so let's preserve that which makes it special before it is lost forever.

Ben Powell is the Editor of *Sidewalk* magazine.

Signing objection forms
for Long Live Southbank

Blondey McCoy and
Sam Hughes

Importance of Place

The location of the Undercroft on the Southbank, in the centre of the city and alongside the Thames, has been ingrained in the appeal of the spot since its inception. Providing an unrestricted space to skate and to practice other urban art forms in the capital, no matter the time of day or night, ensured its popularity throughout the five decades it has been in use.

Legendary skateboarder Mark Gonzales highlights the appeal of the location in the capital city, saying, 'It's a place where skaters from all over the world can go and meet skaters from other countries and its always been a great place for skaters to unite and it's not a skateboard park which makes it fun and friendly for tourists to… come across, and maybe for the average person, to mingle with skateboarders on a common ground.'

Rod Broomfield, like many skaters, is keen to point out that, 'It's not a skate park, but an area adopted by skaters for its idiosyncratic skating possibilities,' yet for skaters and even roller bladers like Leon Humphries, there was something special about the accidents of architecture that made it the perfect place to skate. Humphries claims, 'The way the banks were angled and the rails positioned captured my imagination.'

Despite the existence of purpose-built skate parks across the city, the main draw of Southbank was that it was not intended for this use. As Lev Tanju, founder of Palace Skateboards, recollects, 'the skaters that skate Southbank skate there because they like that it's not meant to be skated. And as soon as you try and box them all in and make them skate somewhere they're supposed to skate they're going to go and grind something else that they're not supposed to be grinding. It'll be like, once it's a skate park there's rules to it. There's things you can get away with at Southbank because you don't have to sign forms to go skate there.'

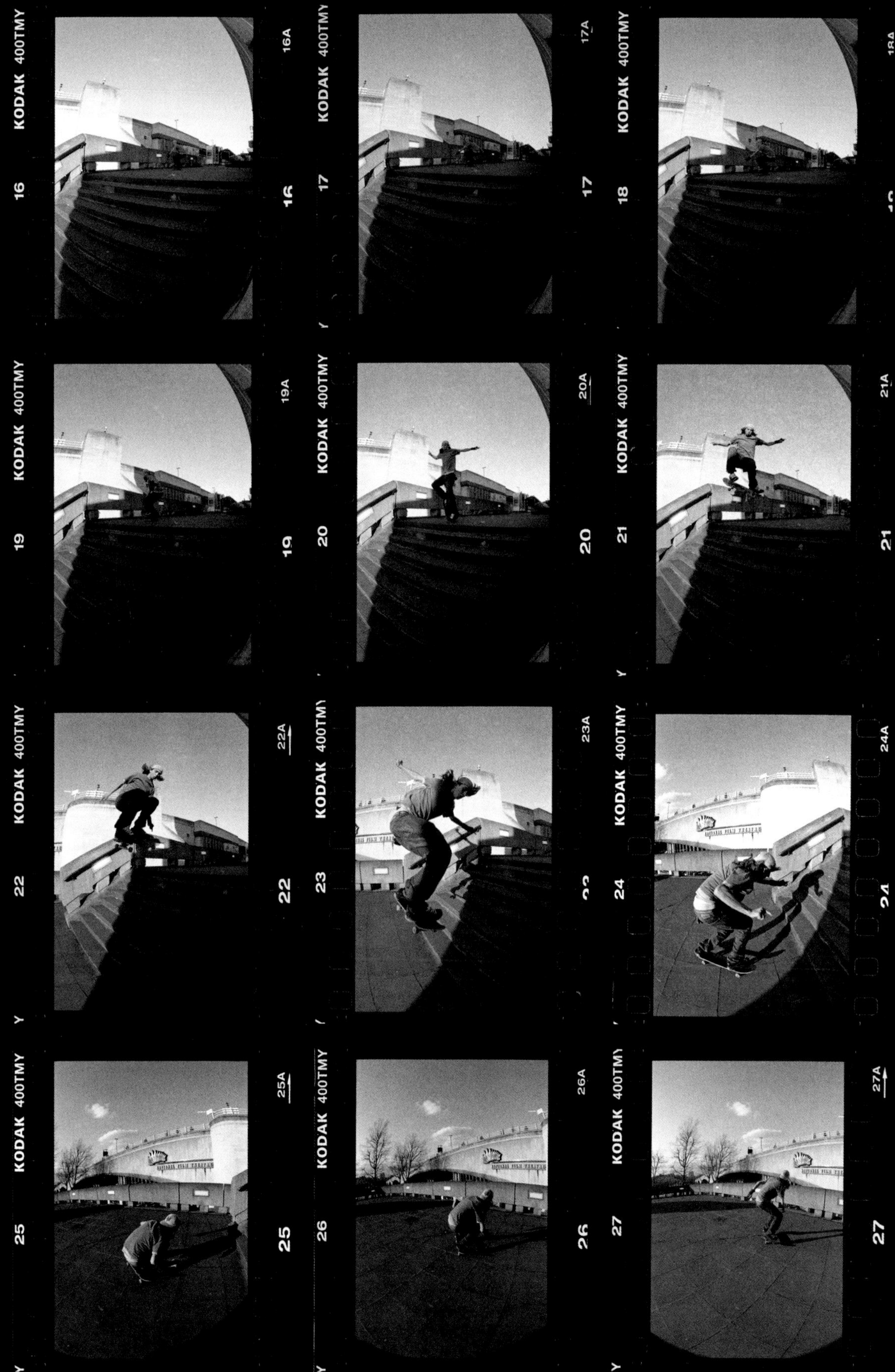

Tom Davies
Fakie Backside 360
2004

Opposite:
Mark Gonzalez

LONG TIME
NO SEE
Thames

Satva Leung
2001

Opposite:
The Long Live Southbank
Campaign Desk
2013

Opposite Top:
Blondey McCoy
2013

The importance of Southbank as a 'found' location further consolidates the impression of the space as a hub of creativity. Musing on the setting Rob Broomfield suggests, 'It's a unique location for skaters, in the way it presents skateboarding to the public in a framed theatrical setting, the graffiti acting almost like stage painting. It looks less "everyday" than other skate parks. But more importantly, the location was "discovered" by the skaters, a truly creative act.'

Situated next to a large arts institution, the Undercroft and surrounding skate areas remained a draw for spectators as well as participants, showcasing unscripted street arts. Brian Blodgett tries to capture the appeal of its location, 'Southbank has created a haven for skaters and even admirers to come together and appreciate what real art is, which is only more fitting because of the arts centres it is surrounded by. People coming to see an opera or an art show normally will stop on their way to watch the contemporary art that is being produced by the youth at Southbank, and may leave with an even wider appreciation of what art really can be.'

Chris Pullman, business manager of central London skate shop Slam City Skates, goes into more detail about the uniqueness of the location, saying, 'Just to look at it, to feel the texture of it all the things you've seen on video, the texture of the floor, rolling around, feeling the slabs and how smooth they were polished, how the light comes in and seeing you're right across the river from all of London. Stand out there up on Waterloo Bridge – Big Ben, round to St. Pauls, and then some – that's such a good experience in itself.'

The presence of the Thames alongside the Southbank is a key feature of the environment. Toby Shuall says, 'Southbank represents the river which is just like the middle of the city where it opens up. The bridges and the river and Southbank itself will always be important to me. That's where I grew up. That's my playground.' To some skaters the river lends a particular atmosphere to the skate spot, as Martin Sweeney recollects, 'There'd be times I'd be down here on my own in the evenings and the fog would be rolling in and you couldn't see the end of the course but you'd still skate...'

Long Live Southbank
Campaign Desk
2013

Long Live Southbank
Support T-Shirt

Nick Jensen also sees the river as an important aspect of the Southbank, recognising its role in influencing the journeys skaters take when departing from Southbank. 'I think sometimes you're lost without a place to start,' says Jensen, 'and the fact that it's on the Thames… and you can see all these buildings, that you know that that's the adventure, you're always going to go eastwards down the Thames. And so we'd always start at Southbank and then go on missions, find new things, skate them, and then return. Its situation, its place, being next to the Thames as well, it's so important as well. It promotes this idea of adventure.'

Toby Shuall describes it as a 'mellow place… basically a park with no trees,' while Jensen urges doubters to see how compelling the place is for the people who skate there, 'It would be beautiful if for once someone would recognise that Southbank is like a park, that it's green to us. The same as a lake to a duck. It's a natural space. It's not like a swimming pool for a duck that's next to the lake.'

Jensen attempts to articulate how this 'dead' space amidst the Brutalist architecture of the area provided some 'magic' for people looking for new skate spots: 'Basically the climate here is shit and the skate spots aren't as good so when someone designs an art gallery and it happens to have dead space, like a thoroughfare – that is what Southbank is – that's then skateable, you've instantly got magic straight away because you've got something that wasn't designed to be something that's very much good for something. And in America that re-appropriation started with skating [Californian bowl-shaped swimming] pools. But this was a full architectural site in the centre of London. And I think the attitude of skateboarders was: you just have to make the most of it. In England the weather's shit and the skate spots aren't that great.'

UNLIMITED

Poetry of

Nick Jensen
2003

Jacob Sawyer
Bigspin Flip
2003

Unknown Skateboarder
5-0 Grind
2005

Above:
Nick Jensen

Opposite:
Neil Urwin
Frontside Heelflip
1995

The Legend of Southbank

Over the last 40 years, the Southbank Undercroft has built up a reputation as a skate spot of international renown. It has been featured in countless magazines and videos, and more recently in best-selling computer games such as *Tony Hawk's Pro Skater*. For four decades, the spot has attracted skaters from across the UK and from around the world, who have flocked to skate its famously unforgiving banks. It is a space that has been shared by people of all ages and backgrounds, where young aspiring skaters getting on a board for the first time can rub shoulders with seasoned professionals.

Over the decades, the Undercroft has achieved legendary status, becoming a magnet for young skaters. 'Our trips to Southbank were a pilgrimage,' remembers Oliver Penning. 'It was a rite of passage for us as young British skateboarders, and to be able to contribute in a miniscule way to that spot and that Great British scene was an enormous deal for us at the time.'

The formidable reputation of Southbank provided budding talents with a powerful incentive to improve their own skills. 'We knew from quite an early age that there was this place Southbank,' recalls Nick Jensen, 'We decided – made a pact – to spend two years working out how to skate. Until we could do a kickflip we wouldn't let ourselves go to Southbank.'

Knowledge of the Undercroft has been passed on from generation to generation of skaters. 'I knew what it was, I'd seen pictures in magazines,' Joey Pressey remembers, 'and then around Christmas time, my friend's parents were going to take us Christmas shopping around Covent Garden and stuff so we took our boards. We got to Slam [City Skates] and Seth [Curtis] was outside. We were desperate to find out where Southbank was, so he took us there. We skated down through Leicester Square and Trafalgar Square and across Embankment Bridge and that was just amazing.
We couldn't believe our luck that this amazing dude that worked in Slam City was taking us through the streets and showing us where not to buy pizza and doing ollies over drains and we were just from a little town in the countryside.'

CREAM

It was not uncommon for skaters to travel great distances in making the pilgrimage to Southbank. Barrington Jeffrey remembers the sacrifices he made to make the trip: 'I was living with my Mum in Wales and I always saw Southbank and always wanted to skate Southbank but never knew I could get here. I found out my dad was living in London. I was like, "Right." I phoned him up hadn't spoke to him in years, I was like, "Dad can I live with you?" He said, "Yeah come on son, come over!"'

Another skater growing up in the south Wales valleys, Chris Pullman, also remembers the lure of Southbank in comparison to the far-off skate spots featured in American magazines. 'You have all the American magazines and everything there seems so inaccessible, whereas the British scene seemed more accessible and easier to reproduce,' he recalls.

Whereas the Californian sunshine seemed to belong to another world entirely, the gloomy concrete of the Undercroft, as portrayed in British magazines such as Tim Leighton-Boyce's *R.A.D*, brought skateboarding culture much closer to home. 'The skateboarding in Britain – it meant a lot more to us than the American magazines where the sun shone all day,' explains Pullman. 'Tim did a good job of making a magazine that was inclusive for us guys. As a result we all wanted to go to London and meet Curtis McCann and meet Will Bankhead, and skate Southbank and Kennington and Stockwell. So the aspiration for kids out of town was huge from then. It was a dream to go to Southbank from a real long time ago. You'd watch videos and spend hours, thinking what you would do if you went there.'

The desire to skate Southbank was equally powerful to skaters living overseas who were exposed to the photographs of legends skating Southbank. For Greg Finch, growing up in South Africa, the Undercroft took its place in a global pantheon of fabled skate spots. 'We knew of all the important spots around the world,' he remembers, 'whether it was EMB in San Francisco, Love Park in Philadelphia, the Bowl on the beach in Marseille, France or Southbank, London, England. We knew almost every inch of these spots because of videos and photos in skate magazines, even though we'd never been there. We studied them and imagined what it would be like to skate these spots. These spots are the reason skaters travel. Southbank, one of these legendary skate spots, is the reason why so many skaters visit London every year.'

Chris Pullman

One day, I think either work was getting me down, or trouble with a girlfriend or money, something was going wrong anyway. My one constant and passion in my life has been skateboarding. It must have been an early lunchtime, I went to Southbank and skated around and was hammering around getting the aggression out and doing what I did and knocking out all the tricks I do, and I did something and I absolutely ate crap, like fell on the floor, lost my glasses, I was just lying there, just kinda half underneath and half not underneath. I just lay there for a minute, looking up at the sky. The trees were green, the concrete was grey, the sky was blue and you could hear the river and the people, and I was lying there just thinking: "It doesn't matter what else is going on with my life, but I'm skateboarding and even though I'm lying here in the dirt, this is such a perfect moment." I was sitting there staring at the sky, I can still picture it now: the sky was framed above me and a head popped into my line of view, really recognisable face. The guy was like, "You ok mate?" and I was like "Yeah man, I'm really good," and I took a second glance and it was Nigel Planer from *The Young Ones*! It was really weird, it was just a surreal moment, I couldn't feel any better.

Rod Broomfield

I've skated on and off for almost 40 years, but what I think I've really enjoyed about the Southbank is seeing the changes. Over the years, I've walked past the Undercroft with my kids and watched the ebb and flow of new young skaters discovering skating at the Southbank.

Barrington Jeffrey

It was the best time of my life when I think about it. Southbank was the best time of my life.

Matt Gold

Southbank is a symbol of all that is special about skateboarding. It is a place in the city where you can go at any time without pre-arrangement and meet like-minded people to play, practice, socialise and generally have fun. It is still one of the only free places to skate in London that is protected from the elements and is known worldwide as the centre of London skateboard culture. There are so few free spaces in London that allow people to engage in self-driven creative expression. It is also important to fight the ever increasing spread of bland corporate capitalist culture that is ruining our society and planet. There is no shortage of places to buy an overpriced coffee and a bagel already within two minutes of the Undercroft.

Southbank Sam

Southbank means everything to me, If I thought they were going to close this place down, I'd chain myself up strap a few *Big Issues* to me, stick a load of rocks in me mouth, tell everybody, "If you destroy it I'll eat the rocks, swallow them, eat loads of sand, please do not knock this place down it means the world to me." Even my daughter comes here now. This is how my daughter got into contact with me, from this place. She found out, "I might find my dad here", and now I've got a good relationship with my daughter and we go out every other day. Without this place I would never have even known who she was.

Southbank is my life, its my life, when this place closes my heart will break, literally.

Aarto Saari

My name's Aarto Saari. I'm a professional skateboarder. I currently reside in Los Angeles, California, and I'd like to lend my voice to save Southbank. I first saw Southbank probably early nineties, when I started skating for videos and stuff, always wanted to go there and got to visit there a few times to ride a skateboard. Southbank is one of the few places left in the world that's been around for a long time and has a lot of history in skateboarding and in the purest form. It's a meeting place: a lot of locals have it for a while and they grow up there, it's kind of their place. I mean: skate parks is one thing, but skate parks don't necessarily breed creativity like places like Southbank do. Where its part of the city, there's people walking around and you're just kind of participating in the community and you're not fenced off somewhere in an area. I think thats whats special about Southbank... because it is more of an art form than a sport. It's a lot more of a cultural thing than just doing tricks and this and that. It's art. That's what bums me out: in a lot of skate parks they kind of take all that away and they kind of mould it into a sport which I don't think it'll ever be... One way or the other skateboarding is going to keep its freedom. Southbank is the perfect place to keep that freedom and make that happen.

Opposite:
Southbank Sam
2013

Alan Rushbrooke
2004

Dan Barnett
2005

Seth's Board
2005

Anderson Marques
360 Flip
2005

Zac

The Southbank Arts Centre as seen from Waterloo Bridge 1967

The History of The Site

Steffan Blayney

The site on which the Southbank Centre sits is at the geographical centre of London. Situated at the corner of a perpendicular bend in the river Thames between the bridges of Waterloo and Westminster, it offers views of the Houses of Parliament to the West and St. Paul's Cathedral to the north east. Home to the Royal Festival Hall, the Queen Elizabeth Hall, the Purcell Room and the Hayward Gallery, it is Europe's largest centre for the arts. Neighboured on its downstream side by the National Theatre and Tate Modern, and attracting more than 25 million visitors annually, the Southbank is the cultural heart of the British capital in the twenty-first century. Until relatively recently, however, the transformation of the Southbank, from marshy countryside to industrial wasteland to world-class arts destination, would have been hard to imagine.

From Lambeth Marsh to the Blitz

The sixteenth-century Southbank. Detail from the Agas woodcut map of London (c. 1561) painted in watercolour by Joseph Jones
1749

Opposite:
The Artichoke public house Lambeth Marsh as painted by Paul Sandby
1770

The area now known as the Southbank was for several centuries little more than undeveloped, rural marshland. At the northern tip of the ancient parish of Lambeth, the legacy of Lambeth Marshe, first recorded in medieval taxation records of the fourteenth century, can still be seen today in the names of Upper- and Lower- Marsh Streets, at the back of Waterloo Station. Until the eighteenth century, the south side of the Thames, in contrast to the expanding city across the water and technically a part of Sussex, remained largely undeveloped countryside, with London Bridge the only permanent river crossing until 1750.

Long before its twentieth-century reinvention as a hub of arts and culture however, Lambeth Marsh, free from the restrictive laws and taxes of the city, was a popular destination for Londoners in search of entertainment – though not always of the most respectable kind! In the sixteenth century, the Southbank was the home of theatres and bear-beating arenas, with some evidence to suggest that the area may have been used even further back by Roman gladiators! Samuel Pepys' diaries recall seventeenth century Lambeth Marsh as a favourite spot for late-night eating, drinking and debauchery, with a less-than-salubrious reputation that would stay with the area well into the twentieth century.

By the mid-eighteenth century, much of the marsh had been drained, and transport links with the north bank were improved by new bridges from Westminster and Blackfriars. With the onset of the industrial revolution, the undeveloped Southbank became a convenient place to locate some of London's more unsightly or malodorous industries – at a safe distance from the City. Vinegar distilleries, tallow factories and waterworks all appeared along the river, before the iconic Shot Tower and Red Lion Brewery were erected in the nineteenth century. The first Waterloo Bridge was completed in 1817, while the arrival of the railway at Waterloo Station in 1848, linked by Hungerford Bridge to the new Charing Cross Station in 1864, saw the Southbank becoming increasingly integrated with central London.

In 1905, the decision was taken to house the London County Council (LCC) in a new building facing across the Thames to the Houses of Parliament. In the view of the Labour politician John Burns, the need for a new home of metropolitan government provided a perfect opportunity to 'lighten up a dull place, sweeten a sour spot, and for the first time bring the south of London into a dignified and beautiful frontage on the river Thames'. Completed in 1922, with further additions in the 1930s, the new County Hall, built in grand Edwardian Baroque style, was a further sign that the long-neglected Southbank was playing an increasingly important role in the life of the metropolis.

Up until the Second World War, however, the Southbank remained predominantly an industrial wilderness, all but cut off from the social and cultural life of its northern counterpart. The area was heavily affected by German bombing during the Blitz, and when J.H. Forshaw and Patrick Abercrombie came to drawing up the County of London Plan for the post-war reconstruction of London in 1943, they described an area that was 'depressing,' 'semi-derelict,' and 'lacking any sense of that dignity and order appropriate to its location at the centre of London.'

Forshaw and Abercrombie recommended replacing the area's decaying industry with green spaces and riverside walks, and envisioned the arrival of a 'great cultural centre, embracing, among other features, a modern theatre, a large concert hall and the headquarters of various organisations.' While the proposals were not acted on directly after the war, within five years of their publication plans were afoot that would see them at least partially come to fruition, and which would see the Southbank become, for one summer, the centre of the nation's attention.

The Lambeth Lead Works' Shot Tower (1826) and Red Lion Brewery (1837)
1920

County Hall (1922)
c. 1940

Opposite:
The industrial Southbank
1938

The Festival of Britain

The suggestion of a festival to mark the centenary of the 1851 Great Exhibition was first put forward by the Royal Academy of Arts in 1943. It was not until the end of the war two years later however, owing in large part to a public campaign launched by *News Chronicle* editor Gerald Barry, that the idea truly got off the ground. A government committee was set up to plan an event under the title Festival of Britain 1951 with the Deputy Leader of the newly-elected Labour Party, Herbert Morrison, taking responsibility for its organisation and Barry appointed as Festival Director.

The Festival was to be designed, in the words of Barry, as a 'tonic to the nation', a welcome respite from austerity and rationing for a country still recovering from the traumatic events of the recent past. At the centre of the nationwide Festival would be a grand exhibition, showcasing the best in British art and design and the cutting edge of science and technology.

While a number of locations were considered, including Osterley Park, Battersea Park and South Kensington, as well as the Hyde Park site which had hosted the Great Exhibition a hundred years previously, by 1948 it had been decided that the Southbank would play host to the flagship exhibition of the Festival. The Victorian brewery and the accumulated disorder of riverside wharves and warehouses were all demolished to clear a 27-acre space as a blank slate for the Festival's architects. Less admirably, whole rows of Georgian terraced houses were razed to the ground, with many local residents forcibly relocated. Only the Shot Tower, preserved due to popular sentiment among Londoners, remained as a testament to the Southbank's industrial past.

Less a nostalgic celebration of past glories than a statement of purpose for the future, the Festival represented a chance for the government to set out a new programme for life and society in post-war Britain. While Morrison denied a political agenda, the Festival and the ideals around which it was organised were inextricably associated with the Labour Party. Described by Barry as 'the people's show', the approaching Festival was dismissed by the recently-defeated Conservative leader Winston Churchill as 'three-dimensional, socialist propaganda.'

The self-consciously modern outlook of the Festival's planners was clearly expressed in the design of the Southbank site. In contrast to the bleak, bombed-out landscape of post-war London, the architectural brief called for 'fun, fantasy and colour,' with the Festival's Director of Architecture, Hugh Casson, later recalling

The Festival site
1951

his intention to conjure the effect of 'an extraordinary, huge toy-shop right in the middle of London.'

A team of young architects and designers, under the leadership of the 38-year old Casson, set to work creating a cluster of vibrant temporary structures, contemporary in design and ambitious in scale. The Dome of Discovery, which housed many of the exhibits on a site between Hungerford Bridge and County Hall, was the largest aluminium structure erected to that date and the largest dome ever built. Wells Coates' Telecinema, the first in the world specifically designed to show both film and television, offered visitors a varied programme of specially-commissioned films, enhanced by pioneering use of special effects and 'stereoscopic' 3D. Perhaps the most striking exhibit on display was the 300ft Skylon, a futuristic cigar-shaped steel spire, suspended in an upright position by a network of cables and appearing to hover above the ground. A popular joke at the time likened the floating structure to the British economy, as both had 'no visible means of support'!

Undoubtedly the centrepiece of the Exhibition, and its lasting legacy on the Southbank, was the brand new Royal Festival Hall, built (in something of a rush) in 18 months between 1948–1951. In contrast to the temporary structures that surrounded it,

Royal Festival Hall and the Shot Tower seen from the east 1961

Royal Festival Hall auditorium seen from the upper circle 1951

the Festival Hall was built to last. The bombing of the Queen's Hall in 1941 had deprived London of its principal concert hall, and the context of the Festival was seen by the LCC as an opportunity to provide a permanent replacement. Designed by Robert Matthew and Leslie Martin, the Festival Hall was the first major public building in Britain to be built in the Modernist style, though with an elegance and attention to detail that has seen it withstand the test of time far more gracefully than many buildings of the same period. Clad in Portland stone, with a barrel-shaped copper roof, the Festival Hall presented a smooth gently-curving façade onto the Thames.

Martin's inventive 'egg-in-a-box' design saw the auditorium suspended above ground, linked by staircases to a large foyer area. In keeping with the ideological principles behind the Festival as a whole, the Hall's architects conceived of the wide open foyer space as a democratic meeting place for all, with no separate bars or restaurants for different classes of patron. In addition, the suspension of the auditorium within the four walls of the Hall and encased in concrete had the added bonus of minimising the noise of trains thundering past over Hungerford Bridge. Inside, the Hall was modern through and through, with everything from the furniture and fabric patterns by Robin and Lucienne Day to Hope Bagenal's pioneering scientific acoustics exemplifying the latest in British design and technological innovation (though in the case of the acoustics, not entirely successfully!).

Despite the huge popularity of the Festival, and plans being discussed to extend the life of the temporary structures beyond the summer of 1951, just a few months later the majority of the exhibits that had filled the long-neglected Southbank with colour and life would be consigned permanently to the scrapheap. The October general election saw victory for a Conservative Party keen to distance itself from the left-wing principles with which the Festival had been associated. His contempt for the Festival clearly undiminished, the very first act of Winston Churchill as returning Prime Minister was to issue an instruction to clear the Southbank site.

Et Tu, Brutalism?

Demolition work began in 1952, and by the time of the Queen's coronation the following summer, the site that had hosted the Festival of Britain was barely recognisable. In one corner, the Telecinema had managed to escape the wrecking ball, reopening as the National Film Theatre in 1952, before moving to its current site under Waterloo Bridge five years later. The Festival's Riverside Restaurant, overlooking the Thames at the north east corner of the site, would also remain in place, but the giant Dome of Discovery and other pavilions that filled the site were razed to the ground, the iconic Skylon unceremoniously toppled into the river before being sold for scrap. For over a decade, the nineteenth-century Shot Tower and Modernist Festival Hall stood out as isolated monuments to two very different eras of the Southbank's history, on an empty expanse of grass and pavement (optimistically rechristened South Bank Gardens), stretching from Waterloo Bridge to County Hall.

If the ten years after the Festival were something of a wilderness period for the Southbank, the Exhibition had nonetheless drawn attention to the area as a central London site with potential for development. In 1961, after years of protracted negotiations with the LCC, the Shell oil company began the construction of a new office complex, facing the river from Belvedere Road. The new Shell Centre comprised a collection of buildings either side of Hungerford Bridge and was dominated by a large tower block, at the time of its completion in 1963 the tallest storied building in Britain and the largest office building, by floor space, in the whole of Europe.

By the time the Shell Centre was erected, plans were already underway for another major transformation of the Southbank site. In the rush to complete the Festival Hall in time for the Festival, plans for a second smaller concert hall originally included in the architects' brief had been abandoned due to constraints of space and time in the build-up to the Festival. In 1955, the LCC decided that they would indeed add a second concert hall, as well as an art gallery, on the Festival site. The first drawings, by lead architect Norman Engleback, were submitted in 1957, but it was not until 1961 that the plans, which now also included an additional smaller recital room, were completed. The Shot Tower was at last demolished to make way for the new buildings, while work also began on extending and renovating the Festival Hall. In 1963, construction finally began on what would eventually be named the Queen Elizabeth Hall, Purcell Room and the Hayward Gallery.

The new buildings were designed in an uncompromisingly Brutalist style, displaying exposed concrete panels, with few windows and minimal decoration. Reflecting the contemporary preference for the separation of vehicular and pedestrian traffic, the new buildings were built on multiple levels, with the halls and gallery raised above the ground and linked to each other and to a newly-refurbished Festival Hall – by elevated walkways. The Undercroft below the Queen Elizabeth Hall, a far more expansive space when first built than what remains today, led to a street-level entrance for car passengers.

The Undercroft
1977

The stark angular designs were originally opposed by Hubert Bennett (replacing Leslie Martin as the LCC's chief architect in 1956) who wanted to see the new buildings conform to the smooth lines of the Festival Hall. However, the threat of mass-resignation by Engleback and his team, many of whom would go on to join the radical Archigram collective, meant that the new buildings would remain – in their own way like the Festival structures that had preceded them – a bold and principled statement of the latest in architectural Modernism.

Southbank development
architectural model
1961

Southbank development
architectural model
1970

Southbank development
construction in progress
1964

The Queen Elizabeth Hall and Purcell Room opened in March 1967, with the Hayward opening in the summer of the following year. In 1976, they were complemented, on the other side of Waterloo Bridge, by the monumental concrete towers of the new National Theatre. The following year, to celebrate the twenty-fifth anniversary of the Queen's accession to the throne, the Jubilee Gardens were opened on the former Dome of Discovery site.

The additions to the Southbank of the 1960s and 1970s have left a complex and controversial legacy. While many continue to celebrate the buildings of the Southbank Centre as leading examples the period's architectural avant-garde, for many the dense, unornamented concrete and at times disorientating walkways represent a bleak prospect. While the Festival Hall has remained largely popular with the public since the 1950s, its sixties neighbours have not fared quite so well. In 1967, *Daily Mail* readers voted the new Queen Elizabeth Hall 'Britain's Ugliest Building', while a survey for the *Illustrated London News* two decades later nominated the whole of the Southbank site – from the Shell Centre to the National Theatre – as the biggest 'blot' on the capital's landscape. For one especially irate reader, the Hayward Gallery in particular represented the destruction of London by 'Modernist, internationalist, socialist Brutalism'. For the next 20 years, the history of the Southbank would be dominated by a series of high-profile attempts – and conspicuous failures – to tame the sixties concrete jungle.

The arts complex from Waterloo Bridge
1970

Small concert hall model
1962

Opposite:
The Hayward Gallery with Shell Centre downstream building behind
1970

Arrested Development

For the first two decades of their existence, the Queen Elizabeth Hall and Purcell Room, along with their more distinguished Festival Hall neighbour, were controlled by the Greater London Council (GLC). Replacing the LCC as London's metropolitan government in 1965, the GLC also administered the Hayward in partnership with the Arts Council of Great Britain.

In 1983, the Labour administration of Ken Livingstone, in the democratic spirit of the Festival Hall architects, launched the Open Foyer programme at the Southbank. For the first time in the arts centre's history, members of the public who were not paying customers were allowed to access the buildings throughout the day, use the foyer areas as public meeting places, and enjoy free lunchtime concerts.

By the summer of that year, however, the GLC was facing the prospect of abolition. The re-election by a landslide of Margaret Thatcher (in whose side Livingstone was a constant thorn) enabled the Conservative government to carry through their manifesto commitment to dispose of all (predominantly Labour-controlled) metropolitan and county councils. With abolition complete by the April of 1986, the administration of the Southbank concert halls and gallery was passed on to a newly-established private company, South Bank Board Ltd., acting initially as an arm of the Arts Council, before achieving independence, in 1988, with the creation of 'South Bank Centre' as a registered charity.

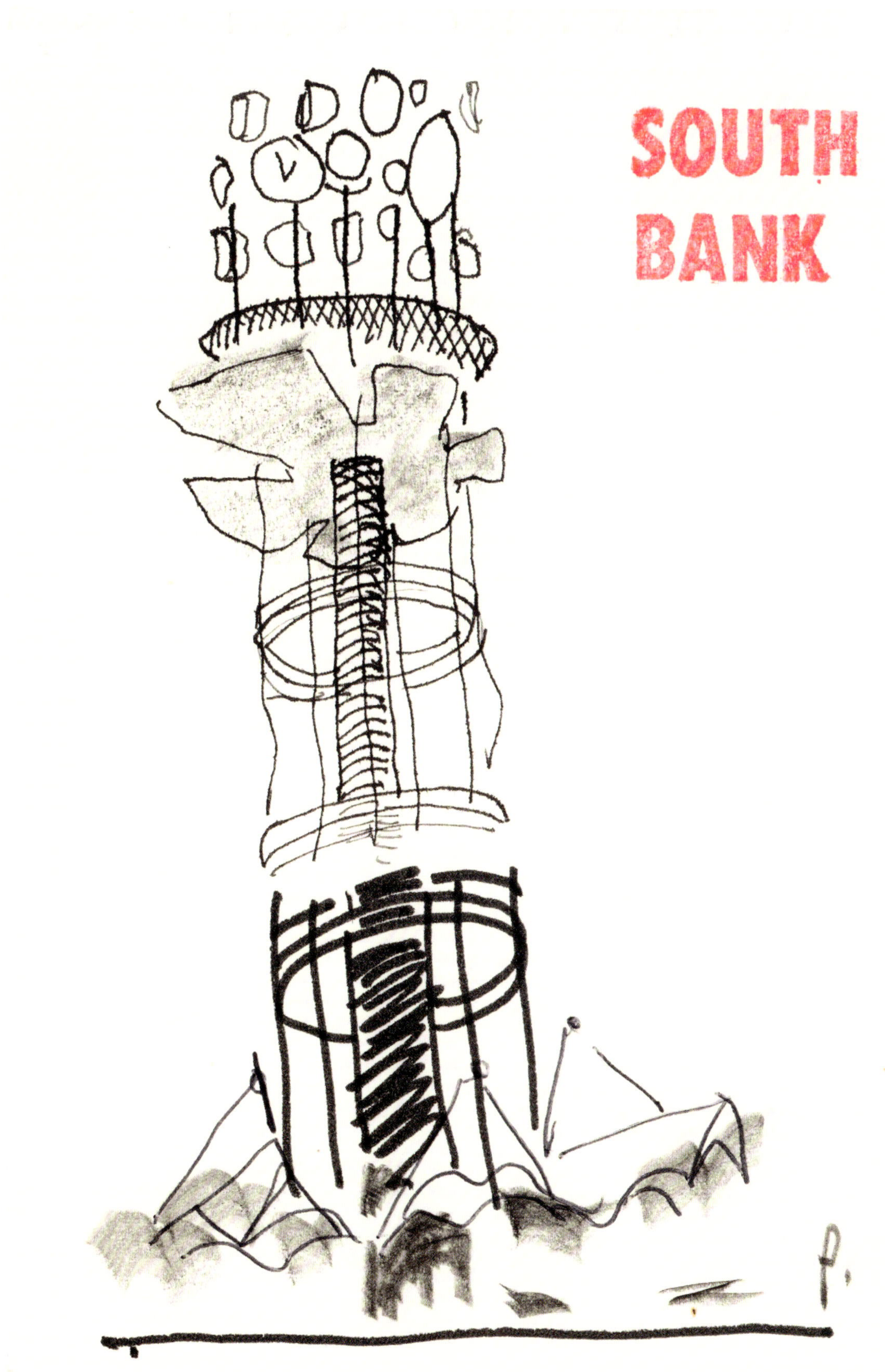

Cedric Price
Perspective sketch
for 'The Thing'
1982–1988

The impending abolition had meant that GLC plans for a revamp of the Southbank under the direction of architect Cedric Price, first publicised in 1983, which would have pre-empted the London Eye by including a giant Ferris wheel on the Thames, as well as a vast spiral observation tower which Price called The Thing , had been scrapped. Under private ownership however, the Southbank would have no more luck in realising the comprehensive overhaul many thought it needed. Throughout the eighties and nineties, a number of extravagant schemes for the area were proposed with great fanfare, only to fall through as a result of a combination of financial and political issues.

Perhaps unsurprisingly, redevelopment schemes tended to focus on the unpopular Brutalist complex of the Queen Elizabeth Hall, Purcell Room and Hayward. Terry Farrell, the consultant architect appointed by the South Bank Board as one of their very first acts in charge, proposed, first of all, to bring the buildings together as a part of a 'shopping and leisure' centre under a giant

Cedric Price
Conceptual sketch on
a photograph of the site
1982–1988

Opposite:
Page 5 *The Times* newspaper
10 March 1989

Jobless are asked to work for nothing in ET pilot scheme

By Roland Rudd, Employment Affairs Reporter

Jobless people are to be asked to work for nothing under a scheme launched by the Government yesterday.

The long-term unemployed will be expected to work free while drawing benefit under work trials being introduced as part of a package of measures announced by Mr Norman Fowler, Secretary of State for Employment.

It is the closest ministers have come to introducing workfare – compulsory work for the long-term unemployed.

Mr Fowler said: "Work trials will offer people short periods of work experience with potential employers while they remain on benefit, allowing employers to reassure themselves about employing people who have been out of work for some time".

The changes to the Employment Training programme announced yesterday also include a job interview guarantee and the funding for 10 school and industry compacts in the inner cities.

The industry-backed Full Employment UK, which welcomed many of the other government announcements, said that work trials would be seen as a "work for the dole scheme" if it is introduced as an alternative to ET.

Mr Peter Ashby, director of the employment group, said: "Unless ministers restrict work trials to ET they will jeopardize the whole programme. It will not be just a cheap labour scheme but a free labour scheme."

Ministers denied the move was tantamount to workfare.

Mr Michael Meacher, Labour spokesman on employment, said: "The new work trials when combined with the 'actively seeking work' requirements of the Social Security Bill spell the end of the current benefit system and its replacement with what can only be described as forced labour.

"Mr Fowler clearly states that the initiatives are to reassure employers and tailor government policies to meet their needs. I doubt that most employers want poorly trained, short-term, unwilling workers, even at nil cost".

Mr Fowler also disclosed that the new training and enterprise councils, run by local employers, will have the power to extend ET to those who have been out of work for three months.

That will increase the numbers on the programme although independent employment groups fear that those who have been out of work for one to two years could be neglected.

Employers in 20 inner city areas are to offer "job interview guarantees" to long-term unemployed.

The Government will also provide up to £50,000 for development work on individual compacts between school and industry, and up to £100,000 a year, for four years, to guarantee young people from inner city schools some form of work and training.

In addition, £3.25 million will be spent on further initiatives to take accout of specific inner city needs.

● A decision by the Ministry of Defence to move its quality assurance department from London to Teesside was welcomed yesterday as an important step towards the regeneration of the region. The move will create 1,500 jobs with the prospect of 5,000 more in support services.

New look for the South Bank Centre

How London's South Bank Centre may look: a model of the latest scheme, by the architect Terry Farrell, looking from the Victoria Embankment

By Simon Tait, Arts Correspondent

The South Bank Centre is to be transformed into the world's biggest integrated arts complex at a cost of £200 million, it was announced yesterday.

In the scheme, by the architect Mr Terry Farrell, the high level walkways will be torn down and new entrances created at ground level. Riverside cafés, restaurants, pubs, and new exteriors will hide the drab concrete of the Hayward Gallery, Queen Elizabeth Hall and the Purcell Room, to "complete the vision of the South Bank as a vital component of the life of central London", Mr Ronald Grierson, chairman of the South Bank Board, said .

"The high artistic standards which have always been set in the activities on the South Bank will be matched from now on by the creation of a lighter environment, an environment which we expect to be rich and varied".

He said a Gallup survey was to be held to find out what facilities the public wanted; planning permission would be sought next month after those views had been assessed. Work would start in 1990 with a hoped-for completion in 1993.

The plans include a new building providing rehearsal and recording studios, a cinema, three storeys of underground parking, a "Discovery Bowl" for outdoor arts activities, and two storeys of office space. It will be built on the Jubilee Gardens site which was once proposed for a 3,500 seat dance theatre – an idea rejected by the present owners, the London Residuary Body. There are no proposals for one in the South Bank plans.

The money will come from Stanhope Properties, who will lease the site from the South Bank in a profit-sharing basis which Mr Stuart Lipton, chief executive of Stanhope, decribed as a "flying carpet leasehold". He said different architects would work on different parts of the project, with sculptors, stained glass artists and craftsman blacksmiths providing original works of art in the exteriors. Mr Farrell would be in an overall co-ordinating role.

To avoid extra costs and disruption to arts programmes, Mr Farrell proposes a dramatic wrapping of the Hayward Gallery, Queen Elizabeth Hall and Purcell Room in a new terraced building, which would also provide extra space for foyers, backstage facilities and viewing balconies.

The Festival Hall itself would remain unchanged (it is a listed building), and there would be complementary recollections of the 1951 Festival of Britain which had turned an industrial slum into a cultural centre.

To help the public consider the proposals, an exhibition in the Festival Hall foyer details the plans.

● Plans for a huge extension to the National Museum of Photography, Film and Television at Bradford, West Yorkshire, which would double the space for public use were unveiled yesterday.

Dealers gather for the fine art fair

SALEROOM

by Sarah Jane Checkland
Art Market Correspondent

A hundred top quality art and antiques dealers are massing at Maastricht, Holland, as stall-holders at the European Fine Art Fair which runs from tomorrow until March 19.

The fair offers an unusually united front for a community normally at professional loggerheads, and apprehensive about increased competition after 1992.

At Maastricht there is a wide range of work, from Old Masters to Impressionists and contemporary paintings sculpture, furniture, clocks, porcelain, armour, jewellery and manuscripts.

Highlights include, for 1.3 million Dutch guilders (about £360,000), "The Robing of Esther", at the stand of the Amsterdam dealer, Dr John Schlichte Bergen. It is by Aert de Gelder, a pupil of Rembrandt who may be responsible for some paintings attributed to that master, and recently "demoted".

Colnaghi, the London dealers, is offering a rare mid-fifteenth century Provencal portrait of a man with a rosary and a scorpion brooch for £300,000, while Richard Feigen, an American dealer based in London and New York, who is a newcomer to the fair, offers a small *grisaille* or monotone painting by Van Dyck: "Rest on the Flight into Egypt" for $650,000 (£400,000). It is related to a painting by Van Dyck in the Queen's collection.

Further competition for London, traditionally the fine art capital, is coming from Paris, where the auctioneers have increased turnover by 30 per cent in 1988, to Fr 2,868 million (£261 million).

In London, buyers were interested in frames not art at Bonhams. Yesterday was a near sell out, with very high prices. A Venetian sixteenth century gilded tabernacle example, its central panel cast with classical figures and flowering urns, fetched 10 times its estimate at £19,800 – a world record for a frame.

John Dunstall, a humble seventeenth century school teacher, overtook Constable and Turner when a page of his delicate studies of walnuts and hazelnuts fetched £73,700 at Sotheby's. The estimate had been £6,000 to £8,000, and the buyer was Agnews. A French buyer paid £44,000 (within estimate) for "Antiquities of Pola," a watercolour by J M W Turner into which three classical monuments crowd. An anonymous buyer spent £41,800 on a sketchy watercolour by Constable of East Bergholt.

Top price at Sotheby's medal and coin sale was £23,100 (four times estimate) for a 1665 medal by John Roettier.

Letters, page 17

glass roof. When these plans fell through, he proposed a new £200m scheme, backed by a large property firm, to 'wrap' the halls and gallery within a new terraced building facing the river. When planning permission for this design ran into difficulties with Lambeth Council, he finally proposed (perhaps out of frustration) razing them to the ground, to be replaced by entirely new constructions on the Jubilee Gardens site, although the collapse of the property market with recession in the early nineties eventually put paid to the redevelopment.

In 1994, a new plan, this time with Richard Rogers at the helm, envisioned a 'South Bank Crystal Palace', enveloping the arts buildings within a giant 'glass wave' sweeping from Waterloo Bridge and around the Festival Hall. In 1998 however, this too would be abandoned, when the Centre failed in their protracted quest to win National Lottery funding.

By the turn of the millennium then, the Southbank buildings had seen off the challenges of three of the most prominent British architects of the era, their concrete façades and snaking walkways remaining defiantly unchanged since their sixties inception.

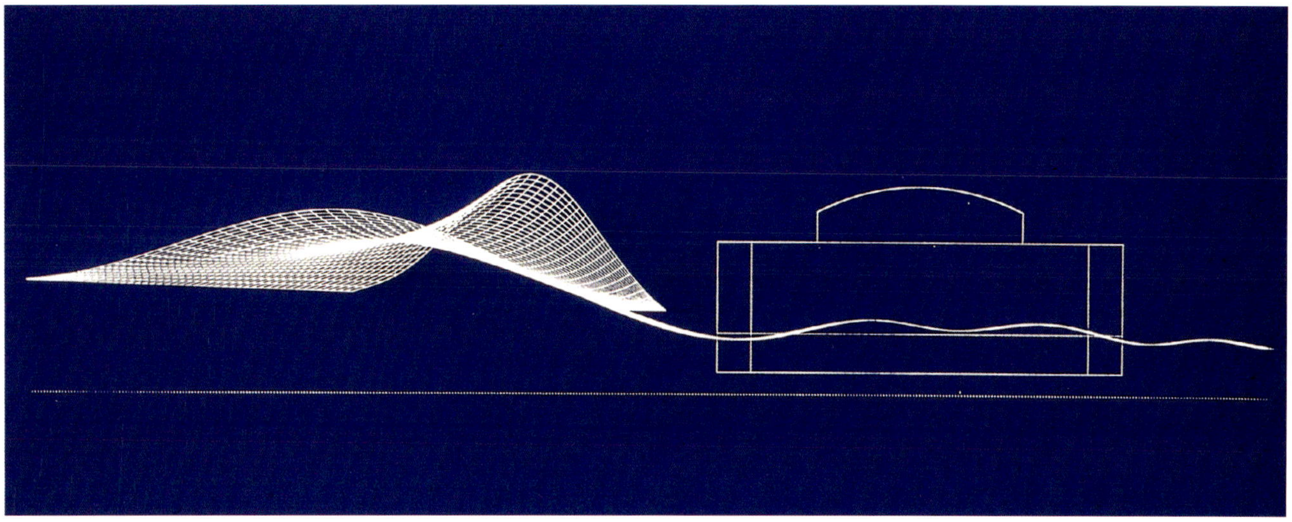

The undulating roof proposed
by Richard Rogers Partnership
1994–1998

The New Millennium

In 1999, the now subtly rebranded 'Southbank Centre' appointed the American architect Rick Mather to the seemingly cursed position of Southbank 'master planner'. While Mather too initially had grand designs for the Southbank, including two new ten-storey office blocks, and the tilting of Jubilee Gardens to make room for new arts and commercial buildings, he was forced to settle for piecemeal development over the next decade. The concrete walkways at the back of the Festival Hall were demolished in 1999, while 2003 saw the arrival of Dan Graham's 'Waterloo Sunset' pavilion attached to the Hayward Gallery.

The coming of the twenty-first century saw a flurry of new additions to the surrounding Southbank. First to come, in May 1999, on the site of the former 'Bullring' roundabout at the end of Waterloo Bridge, was the new London IMAX, boasting the largest cinema screen in Britain. In May 2000, in the former Bankside Power station downstream of the National Theatre, the Tate Modern gallery became the latest addition to an increasingly impressive range of cultural attractions on the river. The new Millennium Bridge, finished the next month, originally linked the gallery to the City of London, but was closed after only two days – not to reopen until 2002 – due to a notorious 'wobble' experienced by the first pedestrians to cross it. The London Eye was erected in 1999, and officially opened by Prime Minister Tony Blair on 31 December in time for the new millennium celebrations. While technical problems meant that the wheel did not open to the public until March of the following year, it has since become the most popular paid tourist attraction in Britain, with over 3.5 million visitors annually.

In the summer of 2005, the Festival Hall closed for a major programme of refurbishment, reopening two years later along with a new office building for the Southbank Centre on the 'Festival Terrace' between the Hall and the railway bridge, as well as new shops and restaurants at the front of the hall facing onto the river. A multi-million pound redevelopment of Jubilee Gardens was completed in May 2012, in time for the Olympics and Queen's Diamond Jubilee, transforming the flat grassland in front of the Shell Centre into a landscaped park with trees, sculptures and a children's playground.

The Southbank has come a long way from the medieval mud flats of Lambeth Marsh. While the jumbled assortment of twentieth-century architecture from County Hall to the National Theatre can at times seem incoherent, the area has provided a unique setting for arts and culture – both authorised and unofficial – over the past half-century. Never the result of a grand unifying design or plan, the composition of the Southbank site today, like the use of the Undercroft for skateboarding, BMX and graffiti since the 1970s, is the result of accident, improvisation and spontaneous creativity.

Royal Festival Hall and
London Eye by night
2008

Illustration by
Daniel Clarke

The Architecture

Iain Borden

When the complex of the Hayward Gallery, Queen Elizabeth Hall and Purcell Room – now referred to by the Southbank Centre as its 'Festival Wing' – was first dreamt up in the early 1960s, the scheme's architects were a team at the London County Council (later the Greater London Council) led by the Sir Hubert Bennett and Norman Engleback, but also including Ron Herron, Warren Chalk and Dennis Crompton.

Significantly, the last three of these belonged to a radical architecture group called Archigram, (who are now very famous in architectural circles, but back then were just a bunch of young mavericks), and who had all kinds of interesting and radical ideas about architecture and city living. What Archigram believed in was the importance of modern architecture in contemporary cities as something which could be an exciting part of the way people lived their lives. So, for Archigram, this was not architecture as glass-and-steel office buildings, as untouchable and sterile objects, as dreary welfare state hospitals and schools designed by faceless bureaucrats and committees, but as something that was full of the mobile, changing, popular and dynamic culture of groovy sixties life. This Archigram architecture (most of it quite fantastical and unbuildable) was exhilarating and multi-coloured, which walked around on stilts, which transformed into different shapes and functions, which you could wear and carry around with you, which even plugged into you and you into it. It was architecture as part of living, breathing, happening urban life, and it was meant to be open to everyone.

It was Archigram's ideas, therefore, which led to the various meandering high-level walkways and open ground-level spaces of the Southbank Centre. In particular, and importantly for skateboarding, there was a very strong idea that some of these spaces should not always be planned for any particular people or activities, but rather that some of them should be simply left open for unpredictable and as yet unknown uses. And so when the Hayward opened in 1968, completing the complex, the architects really – and quite deliberately – had no exact idea about what these uncertain uses might be, and no idea about who would used the Undercroft and in what ways.

The break between the Purcell Room
block and Queen Elizabeth Hall
1967

Opposite:
The high level walkway and segrated
pedestrian system linking the centre
1967

Dave Wilson
c. 1972

Consequently then, when skateboarding came along a few years later in the mid-1970s, it was as the fulfilment of the Archigram architectural promise, providing exactly the sort of unexpected eruption of creativity for which Archigram were hoping. Where the architects had designed flat spaces interrupted by a series of surprisingly and apparently uselessly-angled banks, the skateboarders saw these very same angled banks as providing a freely accessible version of the commercial skate parks, which were then being constructed in London, across the UK and in other cities worldwide. The roof of the Undercroft was of course the other great attraction, allowing skateboarders to carry on with their enjoyable movements relatively sheltered from Britain's all too common rain and winds. Here, under the protective ceiling, up and down the angled banks, and in between the curious Doric-mushroom columns, the skateboarders were free to emulate the surf-style and pool-orientated skateboarding which was then being favoured in the pages of magazines like *Skateboarder* in the US and *Skateboard!* in the UK; they carved along the banks, performed kickturns and tailblocks at the top edges, and generally invented their own unique interpretation of American skateboarding.

The riverside fenestration and pedestrian spaces of Queen Elizabeth Hall at night
1967

The Hayward Gallery main entrance on the upper level
1968

Staircase linking the
Hayward Gallery's upper
and lower galleries
1968

As all this suggests, this is much, much more than just the history of a building as concrete structure, and is also the history of what people have done with that building. As French philosopher Henri Lefebvre has argued in his seminal book *The Production of Space*, architectural and urban space is made up of three things: the physical places which we use (in this case the Brutalist concrete and space of the Southbank Centre), the conscious ideas that we have of buildings (such as the designs by the architects), but also, and very importantly, people's actual uses and experiences of buildings. In addition, as Lefebvre also argues in many of his other texts, it is the everyday lives of people that are really the most important part of our cities and histories – not grand monuments, huge spectacular sporting events or imposing institutions, not individually famous generals, sports stars or politicians, but what we do with our bodies, who we talk to, who we love, how we think, how we feel, what we truly enjoy and value.

And so the history of skateboarding in the Undercroft space is also absolutely part of the history of the Southbank complex, not as a history of this architecture as a static monument, or as a great invention by creative architects, or as a symbol of the legacy of the Festival of Britain, but as a place where people, in this case skateboarders, have done something with their own bodies and ideas, and have created something that is actually kind of extraordinary in its dynamic expression of youthful energy and joy.

Queen Elizabeth Hall and Purcell Room as seen from the upper pedestrian level opposite 1967

One of the access bridges
of the Hayward Gallery
2009

Nor is this just the case of skateboarding being an isolated or short-lived moment in the history of the Southbank. Rather, skateboarding has now been taking place in the Undercroft space for nigh on forty years, making this what is very probably the oldest place in the world that has been subjected to skateboarding continuously and intensively throughout this period.

Just how intensive that skateboarding usage has been is particularly evident during the 1980s and 1990s. In these years, after many skate parks had closed down at the end of the 1970s, skateboarding became much more of a street-based activity, in which skateboarders used the ollie in order to move up on to the ledges, benches, planters, handrails and other street furniture of everyday city streets. The Undercroft changed too, becoming now much less a free skate park and much more like an urban street terrain, somewhere with the character of having been appropriated and taken over by skateboarders for their own purposes and pleasures. It changed again in 2004, when the first concrete blocks were added, quickly followed by niceties such as lighting, CCTV and a benign police presence to reduce petty crime. Railings and yellow lines were also added to demarcate a skateboardable space. Murals and graffiti also started to arrive at this time, adding to the sense of the Undercroft as a centre for various urban arts, and not just for skateboarding.

Nick Jensen

The Hayward Gallery
1968

Foyer of Purcell Room and Queen Elizabeth Hall
1967

Ramp to the exhibition space of the Hayward Gallery
1968

Tom Penny
360 Flip Revert

As result of all this activity and of the space's tolerance of a gradually shifting dynamic, the Undercroft has achieved near mythic status as the epicentre of UK skateboarding, a place where tens of thousands of skateboarders have learned their craft, from novices to professionals, and from hardcore locals to occasional visitors. The Undercroft is then UK skateboarding's most precious home, its original Garden of Eden, its mother ship, its oldest sparring partner and its most famous Wembley Arena – all rolled into one. And of course it is also a place of pilgrimage for skateboarders globally, where tens of thousands have come just to see and roll across one of skateboarding's most hallowed of grounds. If there were to be just one heritage blue plaque put up to skateboarding, it would surely go here.

But this is never a matter purely of heritage and history. If this were the case then a simple museum, a book or a documentary film could stand in for skateboarding. Of course, this is not the case, for the real value of skateboarding lies not in words (like these), or in visual records as movies or photographs, but in the actual act of skateboarding, when someone does that seemingly simple thing and stands on a board, pushes off, and expresses themselves in motion. This movement also takes its meaning from the context in which it takes place – and at the Undercroft we find an extraordinary collision of Brutalist architecture and youthful bodies, where dark concrete, rough textures and echoing acoustics meet splashes of colour, sudden adrenaline and the rasping, grinding, sliding sound of skateboards. These contrasts suggest all kinds of things, not least that the arts are far more than painting and sculpture, that noises as well as music are parts of the sounds of the city, that everyone has a right to have access to public space and to be creative within it, that we should not always have to pay for a coffee or buy something for every moment that we wish to exist outside of our own homes, that great architecture can take unusual and surprising forms, and that people can become urban citizens in a myriad of different ways. Under the belly of the beast, these juxtapositions create amazing lived-in architecture, produce dynamic city spaces, and so meet the theories of Lefebvre and Archigram all at once.

Main entrance and plaza
of Purcell Room and
Queen Elizabeth Hall
1967

Hayward Gallery
1968

Nate J

HAYWARD
ED RUSCHA

Hayward Gallery at night
2008–2009

This is also why so many non-skaters come to the Southbank and to its Undercroft space– people from all over London, right across the UK and the world enjoy seeing the Undercroft's unique combination of skateboarding-against-concrete, and so witnessing a truly public space in action. This is really important stuff, and in many ways it transcends the immediate needs of skateboarding and speaks to a much larger question as to what kinds of public spaces we wish to have in our cities today. In particular, do we really want to have all of our public spaces look like shopping malls, homogenous high streets with their predictable combinations of Yo-Pret-Starbucks? Or would we rather have truly diverse, uncertain, strange, unusual and challenging public spaces – places where all can come, all can see, and all can do?

Skateboarding at the Undercroft suggests that public spaces can be so much richer than the shopping mall. It suggests that different people doing different things can perceive, use and enjoy architecture and city spaces in different ways, It suggests that, in turn, we would like our city spaces to be similarly different and varied, at once loud and quiet, rough and smooth, colourful and monochrome, flat and angled. And, above all, it suggests that we most enjoy cities and buildings when, through the different ways in which they are used by different people, they both comfort and challenge us, when we feel that we can be both relaxed and excited. Skateboarding at the Undercroft is but one small part of this process, but it is a very important one.

Iain Borden is author of *Skateboarding, Space and the City* (Berg, 2001, revised edition forthcoming), and Professor of Architecture & Urban Culture at University College London.

Illustration:
John Horner

QUEEN ELIZABETH HALL
PURCELL ROOM

ROYAL
FESTIVAL
HALL

BiCK
SARO

21 JUNE
musicday.org.uk

Kadir Guirey
1978

Opposite:
Unknown Skateboarder
Freestyle Skateboarding
c. 1973

1970s

During the early 1970s, the popularity of skateboarding exploded in America and by the middle of the decade it had hit Britain in a big way. Early British skaters who were influenced by the exciting pool- and ditch- style skating emerging in California took these moves to the Undercroft and Southbank became a home for the newly formed British skate community.

As skateboarding became more established, skaters experimented with new possibilities and different styles, such as slalom, bank skating and freestyle skating, started to develop as the popularity of the sport grew in the latter part of the decade. From 1975–77 the Undercroft was packed with skaters learning new manoeuvres and pushing the boundaries of their abilities.

Early Days

From early on, the desolate area along London's Southbank made its name as a hub of activity for the burgeoning sport of skateboarding, acting as a breeding ground for new styles of skating and drawing huge crowds.

While examples of primitive skateboards can be found going back to the early decades of the twentieth century, the modern sport has its origins in the Californian surf culture of the 1950s and 1960s. When the waves were flat, bored surfers would nail roller-skate wheels to wooden boards, and keep occupied by 'sidewalk surfing' the beachside pavements, soon progressing to the 'concrete waves' to be found in empty backyard swimming pools, as well as drainage pipes, reservoirs, and any number of other found and appropriated surfaces and spaces.

While remaining largely a west-coast phenomenon through the 1960s, skateboarding enjoyed a brief spell of popularity across the States in the middle of the decade, and in 1965 the *Daily Mirror* reported that 'the biggest craze since hula-hoop' had arrived in the UK. Such excitement was short-lived however, and it was not until the early 1970s – in large part due to the introduction of plastic polyurethane wheels, replacing older steel or clay versions, and allowing for increased grip, control and speed – that skateboarding would really take off, on both sides of the Atlantic.

The Undercroft
c. 1978

Clive 'Manny' Mandersson
of Skate City Team
1977

It didn't take long for the early British pioneers to discover that the idiosyncratic modern architecture of the Undercroft, with its varied levels and sloping banks, its protection from the rain, and prominent central London location, provided the perfect terrain for the new sport, although it would be a while before word spread.

Early slalom pioneer Jim Slater recalls how only around eight people originally started skating the area along the Southbank. In the long hot summer of 1976, however, the sport suddenly exploded in the UK, and the Undercroft population rocketed overnight. 'It started getting rammed quite quickly,' recalls Edwin Brockman, an early Southbank skater. 'Obviously with the summer of 76 being a lovely, gorgeous, hot summer, that's when skating really picked up in London.'

Unknown Skateboarders
1977

Opposite:
The Undercroft
1977

With the buzz around the new sport, Martin Sweeney remembers how 'just about anyone and everyone had a skateboard,' and people began taking to the banks in their hundreds. Many early skaters observed that sometimes it could take up to 40 minutes to do one trick on the banks due to the number of people packed into the Undercroft, such was the intensity of the craze in 1976–77. 'It was like ants going around full speed,' continues Sweeney, 'people travelling around, but no one was bumping into each other, they were just skating.'

The Greater London Council reported numbers of skateboarders at Southbank topping 1,000 at weekends. While a number of local authorities were putting in place measures to ban or deter skateboarding – for example at the Broadwalk in Kensington Gardens, where a resurfacing job put paid to an early skating hot spot – the GLC turned a blind eye, quickly making the Undercroft the centre of the capital's skate scene, and the symbolic home of British skateboarding.

While the 1960s arts buildings at the Southbank were not always popular with the public, many saw this new spontaneous use as a positive development for the area. As early as 1977, press reports were describing the Southbank as a 'haven for young skateboarders,' while many commented that the new use had culturally enlivened a previously underused or unwelcoming area.

'That godforsaken waste-land is good for little else,' observed the Spectator in 1979. 'Is there anywhere, outside a Soviet industrial centre, such a collection of gloomy and soulless buildings as stands between the London Weekend centre and the Hungerford Bridge? Skateboarding would seem to be one of the few rational purposes for those vistas of concrete and paving with curious hidden recesses and – for the skateboarder – challenging ramps… as I walk to the concert, huddled against the wind, I hear the rattle of the boards, some small evidence of human life.'

With the Undercroft beginning to attract attention, the early skaters recall how the spot quickly became the space for new styles of skateboarding to evolve. Chris 'Clingfilm' Linford remarks, 'You've got people doing freestyle, the whole freestyle scene was set up from here. The street scene was all set up from here. Slalom originated from here. So it was pretty much the whole skateboard world as we know it started here.' Rob Ashby remembers how 'everyone did a bit of everything' in the early days, experimenting with multiple disciplines.

Slalom

Tim Panting
Slalom Skateboarding
1978

One of the first areas in which Southbank was to have an influence on the emerging sport was in the discipline of slalom. Slalom is a style of skateboarding that involves weaving in and out of a set of narrowly spaced cones while travelling at high speed. It takes focus and practice to master the right technique.

The smooth concrete flat ground of the Undercroft and its relative isolation from walking traffic meant that Southbank quickly became a popular spot for slalom. In the 1970s, it acted as the perfect training ground for several skaters who would become leaders in the discipline. 'From my era,' remembers Rob Ashby, 'Southbank produced four Slalom World Champions – Paul Price, Michael Stride, Floyd Reid and Martin Drayton – as well as freestyle World Champion, Shane Rouse,' a testament to the level of talent practicing in the Undercroft.

Jim Slater, one of the first big names in slalom and a star of the early skateboard magazines, was also a Southbank regular. 'When I first met him, I used to hide down there behind the columns at the far end and watch him,' remembers Martin Sweeney, 'and then I'd go away to Brockwell Park and practice like mad.' Fashioning cones from items such as beer cans stolen from the bins of the Lambeth Country Show, the slalom skaters would often practice in Brockwell Park, Crystal Palace and Hyde Park before heading to Southbank in the evening once the roller skaters had moved on.

Sweeney, who went on to win all the British slalom championships in the 1980s, as well as some international competitions, claims the distinctive slalom style developed at Southbank was related to the confined space they were training in. 'I think that's why we got into tight slalom,' he explains, 'because the wider the cones the less cones you had so we started bringing them in closer and closer. We went from 6 to 5 to 4 foot centres and then I took it down to three foot. I mean to go through 3 foot you can't believe how fast you gotta go into it. You can't do it slow. You have to absolutely go in like a cruise missile and you can't see the cones as you're going through. It's just a natural rhythm. If you hit one you're out of it anyway.'

The architecture of the space as well as the shelter provided by the roof covering and night lighting helped the slalom skaters to develop all year round. In poor weather, when wheels couldn't grip wet pavements, Southbank offered the possibility to keep in shape and keep skating. Slater points out that 'there were better places, there were hills and there were smoother surfaces, but this was the only one in London you could use in the winter and in the rain and at night. The only one. So it was very, very important for slalom.'

In contrast to other forms of skateboarding, Sweeney feels that slalom provided a more accessible spectacle, becoming a huge draw for crowds at Southbank: 'People could understand that [slalom]. If we were going head to head, like we did down here, we would get people down the side here, hundreds of people and as you would come through the crowds would close in. I mean hundreds, thousands. And they would close in and you couldn't see who won the race because the people would come in and close it all off. It was unbelievable. It was like the waters closing for Moses.'

Chris 'Clingfilm' Linford also remembers the atmosphere on crowded evenings while they practiced slalom: 'The noise of maple slapping the floor. It used to be heaving. I mean, all the little banks at the back used to be absolutely packed. And I remember watching Jim Slater do slalom, where he used to skate this bubble of people. So many people watching, people would just part the way and he could only see one or two cones ahead. It just used to have thousands of people here.'

Freestyle

Freestyle skateboarding is a technical form of skateboarding performed on flat ground. Early freestyle skaters in the 1970s performed handstands, manuals, and other technical tricks. The smooth, undercover arena of the Undercroft provided an ideal location for freestyle skaters to develop their art, offering a dry environment in which to practice their complex manoeuvres.

Some of the earliest moves to come from freestyle skating exhibited the emerging sport's debt to surfing. Many of the early tricks that developed were direct emulations of surfing manoeuvres. One such move was the hang-ten nose manual, in which the skater stands with both feet on the nose of the board, lifting the back wheels off the floor and balancing the board on two wheels.

The Undercroft's large skateboarding community provided freestyle skaters with an atmosphere conducive to experimentation. The skaters pushed each other to learn and invent innovative new tricks. As the 1970s progressed, the Undercroft saw one-foot manuals, longer 360 spins and handstands on double-stacked boards, as freestyle skaters constantly expanded the boundaries of their new art.

Unknown Skateboarders
Freestyle

Danny Acton-Bond
Space Walking Freestyle
1978

Bank/Transitional

The 1970s was the decade in which the Zephyr Competition Team, better known as 'Z-Boys', came to prominence in the world of skateboarding. The former surf team, from Santa Monica, California, which included stars such as Stacey Peralta and Tony Alva, was hugely influential on the development of the sport. Inspired by their impressive, aggressive, surf-influenced style – gleaned from the pages of magazines and the first early films to cross the Atlantic – many British skateboarders broke away from traditional freestyle and became drawn to transitional, bank-style skateboarding.

Skateable outdoor pools, where the Z-Boys plied their trade in California, were virtually non-existent in the UK. At Southbank however, London skaters wishing to imitate their American heroes had a readymade substitute. While the mid to late 1970s saw the arrival of the first few purpose-built skate parks in London, such as Meanwhile Gardens and Stockwell, the 35-degree angled banks of the Undercroft provided the perfect terrain for skaters to emulate the surf-style transitional skating that the Z-Boys had introduced, completely free of charge.

One of the pioneering moves from this period was the bert slide, named after Larry Bertlemann, a famous American surfer. The skater puts their hands down on the transition surface as the board carves , performing a 180-degree slide, before regaining balance as they ride off the bank.

The banks were key to Southbank's popularity during the 1970s, providing a slice of the Californian experience in London, and vastly expanding the possibilities open to skateboarders. On the 'small banks' and 'big banks' of the Undercroft, skaters were able to hone their technique and learn a variety of new tricks.

Unknown Skateboader
1977

Opposite:
Unknown Skateboader
1978

John Crace
1977

Dave Wilson
1975–79

Tim Levis
1978

Unknown Skateboarder
1977

Opposite:
Unknown Skateboarder
1977

The Undercroft
1977

Unknown Southbank Local
1975–79

Unknown Skateboarder
1977

Roller Skating

It wasn't just skateboarders who saw the possibility in the smooth surfaces and all-weather surroundings of the Undercroft. 'A lot of people don't mention this because of the skateboarding,' explains Martin Sweeney, 'But you also had the buzz of roller skaters here from '79 to '83 taking over. Absolutely as many roller skaters as there were skateboarders at the beginning.'

The space was shared amicably, with an informal arrangement that the roller skaters would be in the Undercroft during the day while the skateboarders would use the smooth paths at Hyde Park, returning in the evening to 'take it over again'.

Andrew Trayt
1981

Graham 'Mac' Maceachrun
and Martin Sweeney
1982

Jackie
1981

Frank Wheeler and
Martin Sweeney
1982

Martin Sweeney
Slalom
c. 1982

Martin Sweeney
c. 1982

Phil The Punk
c. 1982

A Growing Community

As skateboarding continued to grow at the Southbank, a community of regulars began to form. While the close-knit group could often appear daunting to outsiders, their outlook was inclusive. As Chris 'Clingfilm' Linford puts it, it was 'very intimidating if you wanted to approach it,' but 'very friendly and open once you're there.'

From the early days, there was a diverse community skating Southbank. 'Back then in the 70s when we first came down, a lot of us were mixing with people we wouldn't have even dreamt of,' remembers Rob Ashby. 'Every race under the sun was coming down and you all were one, and there was no bad feelings to anyone. You just all got on because you were skaters, first and foremost.' 'There was no racism,' agrees Linford, 'It didn't matter how much money you had, didn't matter about your background. Didn't matter who you were. You were a skater. If you were wearing Vans you were in.'

Early Southbank skaters remember a varied scene, made up of skaters from different disciplines, but grounded in mutual support and respect. 'If somebody pulled off a really good trick, you won't find any jealousy,' explains Jim Slater, 'Everyone'll all cheer and clap, and that still happens to this day. What was great about it was the sheer numbers of us, and there was always someone to look out for you. If anybody fell off and got injured there was always someone with a first aid kit, there was always encouragement.'

The unique draw of the Southbank meant that many of the famous faces featured in the emerging skating press could often be spotted in the Undercroft, in turn increasing its attraction for ordinary skaters. 'We would always head up to Southbank to see what was going down and maybe to catch a glimpse of a "famous skater" from the magazines,' remembers Rob Ashby. 'The magazines were good but there was no substitute for seeing one of your heroes tearing up Southbank in the flesh, so to speak. It also made it easier to work out the latest tricks if you could see first-hand how they were done, rather than relying on magazine photo-sequences.'

A group of Undercroft regulars joined together under the name LSD: 'London Skates Dominate'. Ashby remembers that the crew was open to anyone, although initiation procedures could be daunting. 'You'd have Floyd Reid standing there saying, "Well you've gotta jump in the Thames if you wanna be one of us." They tried that on me when I first came up here. But it was basically just come down and skate. The more times you came down the more you got known. You proved yourself. It was kind of a rite of passage. As long as you could skate, you were one of the crew.'

Unknown Skateboarders
Freestyle

Russ Howell
Freestyle Spin
1978

Unknown Skateboarders
Freestyle

Unknown Skateboarder
1977

Steve Kane
Double Kickflip
1978

A Home

The lack of facilities available to skateboarders in the early days of the sport meant that skaters had to improvise as much as possible. Public parks, pavements and playgrounds were often the only spaces available in which to practice.

As Chris 'Clingfilm' Linford remembers, skaters' creative uses of public architecture often made them unpopular with the authorities, with the new sport targeted from the start as 'too anarchical'. Across the country, local councils adopted a hostile attitude to skateboarding. By 1978, two of London's most popular spots had been taken away. The sport was banned in Greenwich Park, while the London Borough of Kensington and Chelsea spent £2,000 on resurfacing the popular Broadwalk at Kensington Gardens with unskateable gravel. In the same year, the Home Office reported that it was receiving 'dozens of enquiries' from local authorities interested in introducing anti-skating bye-laws.

With skateboarders constantly being moved on or their favourite spots closed down, the pioneers were searching for a more permanent home, and the appeal of the Undercroft was clear from the outset. 'We used to skate in the Broadwalk in Kensington Gardens,' remembers Jim Slater. 'Once it rained, or it was too cold and it was dark, of course we couldn't skate, and then someone said, "Well look, we know this place you could set some cones up and it's on the Southbank." We came here to look and then we were hooked because it's somewhere you can skate in the dark, at night, all weathers, and it became our home.'

Between the drab concrete pillars of the Undercroft, skaters found a beauty that few others could appreciate. 'This place would have a shine on it just from the urethane,' recalls Martin Sweeney, 'It was pure smooth. It was just polished from skating. There was none of this graffiti or anything like that. If it was dirty we'd actually sweep it ourselves.'

London's skaters had finally found a place where they could skate all day free from harassment, although the unique appeal of the Undercroft was often lost on outsiders. 'None of my family could understand it,' remembers Floyd Reid. 'What did we do there all day? Who were the owners? How much to skate? When does it open and close? Who makes sure you all wear pads? What happens if someone gets hurt? There were no real answers to any of the questions, all we knew was that when London was soaked with rain, which seemed to be quite often, everywhere was wet, Southbank would be dry and everyone would be there skating during the rain beneath the Undercroft.'

Southbank's growing reputation as the spiritual home of London skateboarding was a major draw for people living outside of the capital. Skaters from across the country were willing to travel long distances in order to get an opportunity to skate the famous banks. Rob Broomfield remembers one such occasion: 'A school trip had been arranged in August '77 to take around 60 skaters the 110 miles from Bristol to London, to the newly opened Skate City – at Tower Bridge – and Southbank. We were incredibly excited at the thought of skating the new park, and finally getting to ride the legendary Southbank, a place we'd only seen skated by the professionals, in the UK magazine *Skateboard!*, and even in the iconic U.S. *Skateboarder Magazine*. When we arrived – a pretty patchy bunch of skaters – we spent about two hours at Skate City, but what I really remember is the ride down the river to Southbank. London was new to most of us, so combine that with heading down the unfamiliar streets to ride a seventies skateboard Mecca – it was a brilliant day. I can't pretend that any of us found it easy to get the hang of the Undercroft's unforgiving banks, but the main thing was being able to go back to the streets of Bristol and say "I've done it, I've skated Southbank."'

Burdette 'Earl' Comefort Fergus
1978

Equipment

While the popularity of skateboarding in the UK was growing at an exponential rate from the mid-1970s, the equipment available to British skaters was severely limited. With all of the main skateboard manufacturers based in the US, quality boards were in scarce supply, and usually out of the price range of most young skaters.

The early pioneers remember fondly their experiments with creating their own kit. Many constructed their own boards, in a similar fashion to the Californian surfers of the 1950s and 1960s, dismembering roller skates and attaching the wheels to planks of plywood. 'I scoured numerous jumble sales for a suitable pair of roller skates to cannibalise,' recalls Rob Ashby. 'I found a pair of "Jacoskates", which I think I paid 25p for. They were fitted with barrel-shaped black rubber wheels with shielded loose bearings. I made the deck out of a piece of marine ply liberated from a rubbish skip and stuck some strips of emery cloth on it for grip.'

The transition to higher quality equipment was a revelation. 'The first time I visited the now-called Undercroft in the late seventies I was sporting a plank of wood attached to a split roller skate,' remembers Stephen Leigh. 'As time progressed and injuries accumulated, the YoYos, Bones, Kryps and Gullwing trucks began to appear. It was like stepping out of a go-kart with flat tires and in to a Ford Escort RS2000 MK1 – every boy racer's dream car at the time.'

By the end of the decade, such products were being more widely manufactured and distributed, and commercial skate gear was becoming available to a greater number of British skaters. While the experimental early days of homemade boards were coming to the end, the advent of better-quality, more durable equipment would vastly increase the possibilities available to skaters.

Rod Broomfield
1977

Dave Wilson
1975–79

Southbank is Our Home!

Paul Price

Illustration by Sam Boxer
2013

LONG LIVE

Act 1 – Why I Skateboard

I can't get enough of skateboarding; I carry my board always and ride everywhere. I depend more time skating than walking. Our PE teacher is a Welsh surfer, so he is letting us skate during some PE lessons.

I do some team sports at school – football and rugby – but I don't like the rules and relying on other people.

I like that there are no rules with skateboarding, and you learn new tricks just by messing around. You need good balance and timing. You just have to go for it. If you hold back or get scared then you can wipe out big time. And it is brutal, I mean when you mess up you slam. HARD! Every Monday I go to school with cuts and bruises after a weekend skating.

It's a totally new sport based on surfing and new tricks are being invented every day. We learn new tricks from skateboard magazines by looking at the photos and trying to work out how they did it. I dream of inventing a new trick because then you get to name it. And designing my own board shape.

It's just new and exciting, like punk. I like a lot of the US punk bands, Devo, B-52s Black Flag, Talking Heads, the Ramones and the Dead Kennedys.

There was a documentary on television showing the California skaters, called *Skateboard Kings*. I hope the BBC repeat it. One of my friend's families may get a Sony Betamax VCR that lets you record TV for up to two hours, but they cost a lot.

Act 2 – Southbank Kids

There's a whole bunch of us that skate at Southbank. It's not a team or gang, just people that turn up. Southbank is great because it is covered and you can still skate when rains, and the lights mean you can skate late.

There are the rich kids, the punks, the posh kids, the poor kids, the drunks, the brainy kids, and the posers. I don't really know much else about my skateboarding mates. Most of us have nicknames. We have skateboarding in common and that's enough. We come from all over London and we call Southbank our home.

We know each other by our clothes. Vans or Nike shoes which are American trainers you can only get at Surrey Skateboards and Slick Willies. No one except skaters have heard of these brands. Someone said they tried to get shoes delivered from the USA but the postage was really expensive and then you have to pay import duty.

If I see anyone in Vans I will go and say 'hello', as it's certain they also skate. My schoolmates wear Dunlop green flash trainers, corduroy flares and duffle coats. We skaters have colourful t-shirts from California, with the design on the back. In *Skateboarder Magazine* I saw skaters wearing Levis 501 jeans, which I found in London at Flip Vintage Clothing in Covent Garden. They are heavy denim and good for skating in. I also have a sky blue and yellow ski jacked which is down-filled and puffy, and the sleeves unzip to make a vest.

A bunch of us went to see the new film *Grease*, which is a musical about American school kids. That school is nothing like my school, and they look really old. Must be all the sun. They had a short playing with it called *Hot Wheels and Big Deals*. It shows Skate City, Southbank, Meanwhile Gardens and Hyde Park. We wanted to see the short again so hid in the toilet so we could sneak back in. When the manager came in five of us stood on the bowl to hide. We saw the film four times in one day. I swear one day I'll go to Australia to meet Sandy Olsen. I feel like I know every line in that film.

I'd love to go to America one day. California looks perfect, pools, parks, sunshine, girls, and surf. Not like Neasden. Not raining like London. At least we have the Southbank.

Nevilla Rada
Freestyle Spin
1978

Act 3 – The Southbank

We can skate Southbank when it's dark and raining. One skater brings his ghetto blaster to play cassettes. There is a handy socket on the wall which saves batteries. Some times he plays jazz funk, which is growing on me, but I prefer punk. It's a 30 watt JVC and is really loud on the tube. I saw on *Tomorrow's World* Sony might soon be coming up with a new personal sound system called a Walkman.

There are a lot of tramps sleeping rough at Southbank. They call it Cardboard City because the tramps use boxes to keep warm. Most of them chat with us during our skate sessions and they all have sad stories. We don't have any money so can't help them. I wonder what the posh people think of Cardboard City as they walk to their shows. They just seem to look the other way and hurry along. As Citizen Smith says, they'll be first against the wall when the revolution comes. The way the Grunwick strike is going it could be soon.

Some American pros came down to Southbank to do a demo. They are so good. I'm going to skate until I can ride like they do.

Anyway, that's enough talk. I want to skate Southbank for a while longer.

I don't want to go home yet. Anyone got 10p so I can call my mum? I want to tell her I'll be skating at Southbank until the last tube.

The End. Of Southbank? I hope not. Save Southbank!

Paul Price has his own signature Professional Model Slalom Skateboard he designed called the Pavel 'Paul Price' Roadster. He now resides in the USA after obtaining the EB-1A 'Alien of Extraordinary Ability' green card for Slalom Skateboard Racing. In the winter he runs the snowboarding company UtahPowderTours.com and teaches snowboarding. He lived in Australia for seven years and blames the film *Grease* for brain-washing him. In the summer he represents Great Britain at major Skateboard Slalom races worldwide. At the US National Skateboard slalom Championships held in California in July 2013 he was 2nd in Tight Slalom and 3rd overall. Whenever he returns to London he skates at Southbank with friends

Dave Smith dissolving into a spin
1978

Paul Price and Chris 'Clingfilm' Linford

Lucian Hendricks
1982–83

1980s

The 1980s saw dramatic changes in British skateboarding, with Southbank central to its development. At the beginning of the decade, skateboarding was suffering from a major decline in popularity. After the initial explosion of the mid-1970s, by the end of the decade the sport was falling out of fashion, with skate parks and ramps being closed up and down the country. Some even went so far as to proclaim that skateboarding was 'dead'. Skateboarding at the Undercroft, however, remained a constant throughout this period, providing a space for skaters to practice their art when other facilities were very limited, and playing an essential role in keeping the sport alive in the UK.

The establishment of the community known as Cardboard City at the Undercroft added another set of users to the space, as did the increase of BMXers on the scene. The different groups learnt to share the space and coexist peacefully, as the various parts of the Undercroft community evolved.

With the privately-run South Bank Board taking over from the Greater London Council in 1986, eventually becoming the Southbank Centre, users of the Undercroft experienced systematic resistance to their presence for the first time, with skateboarders and BMXers alike describing measures that were taken to prevent them from practising in the space. The users of the Undercroft, however, would not let these obstacles stand in their way.

The 1980s turned out to be an innovative and crucial period in skateboarding with the development and growth of street skating. From the middle of the decade, following the release of the popular film *Back to the Future*, the popularity of skateboarding reached new heights, resulting in an increase in the number of skaters, skateboarding styles and general technical progression at the Southbank.

Edwin Brockman
1982–83

Crispin Robinson
1982–83

John 'Bricky' Embury
1982–83

John 'Bricky' Embury
c. 1982

Cone setup for slalom
c. 1982

From Left:
Rob Ashby, Floyd Reid, John 'Bricky' Embury, Dieter Cole, Chris Charalambus, Danny and Graham 'Mac' Maceachrun
c. 1982

The ‘Death’ of Skateboarding

‘In the early eighties,’ recalls Winstan Whitter, ‘skateboarding was pronounced dead’. As a result of this, he continues, ‘the corporate mainstream interest’ in the sport ‘disintegrated swiftly, along with the councils shutting down skate parks left right and centre’, leaving the Undercroft as one of the few remaining London locations used by skaters. To make matters worse, the privatisation of the Southbank arts complex in the middle of the decade saw the arrival of new owners who were openly hostile to skateboarding.

Illustration by
Ged Wells

Southbank Crew

Ruben Goodyear
Backside Boardslide

Tommy Guerroro
1988

Resistance

Opposite:
Rob Ashby
c. 1982

While under the administration of the Greater London Council, skateboarding had been tolerated in the Undercroft, the newly formed South Bank Board, and subsequently the Southbank Centre, took an entirely different attitude.

Winstan Whitter, who was a Southbank regular during the 1980s, describes how the relationship between the Undercroft users and the Southbank Centre 'wasn't so harmonious' during this period. 'They tried to implement a 7pm curfew on the whole Undercroft on a Saturday evening because of their theatre shows. This was due to the performances in the Purcell Room,' directly above the skate area, so 'the noise used to travel up into the main stage'.

Whitter explains that this was when 'the first battle began between them and us,' and describes the Southbank Centre 'throwing stones, pouring water all over the place and having security guards there to kick us out,' among other measures taken to deter skateboarders from using the space.

When the Southbank Centre planned large-scale redevelopment works in the late 1980s, the skate and BMX community were not consulted – or even considered – by the planners, who sought to include the Undercroft within a new arts building that would 'wrap' the Queen Elizabeth Hall and Hayward Gallery. For the first time, skaters began to organise as a unit, joining with local community groups who were opposed to the redevelopment, in an attempt to protect the space they called home. Skaters Gavin Hills and Tim Leighton-Boyce were interviewed by *The Guardian* about the future of the space, while the latter, as editor of *R.A.D* magazine, encouraged a 60,000-strong readership to send written objections to Lambeth Council.

In 1988, the skate community showed their defiance in the face of Southbank Centre threats, when huge crowds turned up to the Smell of Death jam at the Undercroft, organised by 'American' Steve Wilshere. With their space at risk, skaters made the best of a bad situation, using paving slabs that had been ripped out of the floor by Southbank Centre staff as makeshift ramps and obstacles.

Edwin Brockman, Martin Sweeney and Leon Clark
c. 1982

Southbank Centre curfew sign
c. 1982

Will Bankhead

Opposite:
Chris Charalambus
1982–83

Popularity

In spite of such adversity, during the mid to late 1980s, skateboarding enjoyed its second wave of global popularity. Many British skaters were inspired by the daredevil hoverboard antics of Marty McFly in *Back to the Future* (1985) and the skate stunts exhibited by Tony Hawk and Steve Caballero in *Police Academy 4* (1987), with the Southbank being the first place where so many remember skating.

Samuel Holsgrove, otherwise known as 'Southbank Sam' has been skating at the Undercroft for 28 years. He recalls how he first visited the space in the eighties following the release of *Police Academy 4*. 'The whole reason I came here was to skate,' he said. 'My brother went to see a film. It was one of those *Police Academy* movies.' Southbank Sam describes how his brother was inspired by skateboarders, 'Bucky Lasek and Tony Hawk and the crew,' in the film. He remembers how, as a result of this, their mother 'went out and bought him a skateboard, but because my mum is such a nice lady she wouldn't buy one without the other, so she bought us both a skateboard.'

Dieter Cole
c. 1982

Floyd Reid
c. 1982

By the end of the decade, the Southbank Centre's large-scale redevelopment plans had finally fallen through, and with the influx of Hollywood-inspired newcomers now filling the Undercroft, it was becoming clear that the skateboarders would not be easily moved.

Reuben Goodyear and Friends

Opposite:
Sami Davies
1987

Progress

The 1980s saw the advent of the home video, allowing major skate brands to produce a high volume of commercial skate videos. This ignited an increased interest in skateboarding tricks and personalities, which spread internationally. In a much more varied and fast-paced culture than that of the previous decade, tricks advanced more rapidly, different personalities came into the skate game, and the overall number of skaters in Britain began to grow again.

Alongside the advancement of skate tricks, a major factor in the rise in popularity of skateboarding in the UK, and across the world, was the advancement of equipment. The days of homemade boards had disappeared. There were several large American commercial producers of boards, such as Vision, Powell Peralta and Santa Cruz, who created fish-shaped boards. While many of these boards were throwbacks to an earlier era of vertical skating, Southbank skaters used these boards to perform street-style tricks on the banks, and wallrides on the bank-to-wall, while the ollie, invented in the late 1970s by Alan 'Ollie' Gelfand, allowed them to propel themselves down the stairs and onto ledges.

Shops were starting to stock skate gear and BMX magazines were beginning to cover skating. The chief British BMX magazine, *Action BMX* aided a steady resurgence of interest, headed by legendary skate photographer Tim Leighton-Boyce. As skate-boarding achieved greater popularity, the BMX content began to wane in comparison, and, under Tim's editorship, *Action BMX* became *R.A.D*, solely dedicated to skateboarding and the British scene, with Southbank at its centre.

Lucian Hendricks
1982–83

Leighton-Boyce documented a period which is remembered for the progression from an earlier surfer and ramp orientated style to true-street skating, which found its home at the Undercroft. The variations of large and small banks, as well as plentiful street planters, waxed ledges, stairs and banks allowed the skaters to progress both in terms of skill and variety, performing tricks which at this point had only been seen as part of freestyle skate routines, or been done on the coping lip of skate ramps.

Winstan Whitter recalls that 'this was a very progressive time for skateboarding,' and attributes this largely to what was happening in 'the sessions at Southbank'. He describes his experiences seeing well-known skateboarders doing remarkable things in this historic location to further the development of the art form. 'The demos that would happen there were phenomenal. I was there for a lot of it. Seeing Natas Kaupus doing frontside rock n rolls on the bank-to-wall, Rodney Mullen ripping up the freestyle area, the Powell Perelta demo with Mike Vallely ollieing the bollards.'

Ian Scudds, known by most Southbank regulars as 'Davross', remembers being part of the evolution of the sport during this period, including the legendary Smell of Death jam. 'There was guys doing all sorts of amazing stuff,' he tells us, and recalls his own inventions of certain tricks such as the 'rail blunt to fakie', 'indie boneless' and 'kickflip footplant', among others. This was a significant time in the development of skateboarding, with the concrete landscape of the Undercroft's small banks, big banks, stairs and ledges enabling a new wave of technical street style flip tricks to flourish.

Rodney Mullen
Samoan Squat

Rodney Mullen
Yo Yo Plant

Rodney Mullen
One Wheel 360
Late 1980s

Steve Caballero
1988

Opposite:
Shane 'Gappy' O'Brien

Rob Dukes
Rock N Roll

Rob Dukes
Slob Air

Rob Dukes
Frontside Ollie

Rob Dukes
Step off the Block

Cardboard City

In the 1980s, London was hit by a homelessness crisis of unprecedented scale. Rising unemployment across the country saw large numbers of people migrating to London in search of work, with jobs increasingly hard to come by. At the same time, savage cuts to housing and social services by the newly-elected Conservative government left huge numbers of people – including increasing numbers of young, single men and women, and people from ethnic minorities – with nowhere to turn. The combined effect was an explosion of visible destitution on the streets of the capital.

With its covered walkways, undercrofts and underpasses, the area between the Southbank and Waterloo Station provided shelter for an increasing number of men and women during the 1980s. By the end of the decade, it was estimated that on any given night anywhere between 1,000 and 2,000 people could be found sleeping rough on the Southbank. Makeshift structures began to be erected in the Undercroft, as well as at Waterloo's 'Bullring' roundabout, and the community that came to be known as 'Cardboard City' became the predominant image of homelessness in Thatcher's Britain.

The visibility of the homeless community at the Southbank, its central London location, and its proximity to 'high' art and culture at the Southbank Centre made Cardboard City a powerfully charged symbol for the inequalities of the decade. The challenge of Liberal leader David Steel to Margaret Thatcher in 1987 to 'take the time to go and look at the Cardboard City on the Southbank' was a common refrain throughout the decade and into the 1990s, with many politicians and public figures – including Mother Teresa and Princess Diana – as well as a regular influx of newspaper and television journalists, visiting – or sometimes spending the night at – Southbank's Cardboard City.

Soup Kitchen set up in the 'Bullring'
a pedestrian underpass used by
homeless people on London's
Southbank area
1988

Man sleeping in a cardboard box
under Waterloo Bridge
1988

Homeless woman sitting
in bed with dog
1993

Homeless man begging
1993

A man sleeping in the 'Bullring' underpass
1988

While the skaters and other Undercroft regulars still used the space, it was increasingly becoming seen as a no-go zone for a large part of the public, for whom the associations with homelessness were reason enough to avoid the area. Winstan Whitter remembers the 'caved area where all their houses were built out of wood with little front doors' and how there were 'fires down there' and 'lots of dogs around'. He describes the ways in which the different groups that made up the diverse Undercroft community adapted their routines to accommodate each other's needs: 'We had a little system between us, which was not to skate through the back area from the big banks to the four stairs after 10pm' so as not to disturb the occupants of Cardboard City. The skaters using the space felt that this was 'was fair enough because they [the homeless people] lived there!'

Whitter describes how these different factions of the Undercroft community established not only an understanding that allowed them to coexist peacefully, but even an amicable relationship. 'We got to know a few individuals,' Whitter recalls. 'I remember a guy called Paddy who lived there with his dog… My old skater friend James Reid became good friends with Paddy, staying at his place on a few occasions. It was a fairly harmonious relationship between skaters and the local neighbours.'

When the South Bank Board took over the arts centre in 1986, the same private security guards who had been tasked with deterring skaters also set out to make life difficult for the occupants of Cardboard City. Many left the Undercroft for the relative peace of the 'Bullring', outside the Southbank Centre's jurisdiction. In 1994, however, planning permission was granted to the BFI to build the new IMAX cinema in the Waterloo roundabout and the site began to be cleared. While for many Cardboard City had become the closest thing they had to a home, in 1998, Lambeth Council won a court order to evict the remaining occupants so that construction could be completed, and the community was broken up.

Different Skate Styles

As well as accommodating the needs of their homeless neighbours, the skateboarders using the Undercroft had divisions forming within their own group which would also have to peacefully coexist. As the UK skate scene developed during the 1980s, the different styles of skateboarding became more defined. Winstan Whitter explains that in the late 1980s, 'freestyle, slalom, street-style and slash dog style/surf' had all become established as individual styles of skateboarding. He recalls how these different groups existed harmoniously as they all practiced their art at Southbank. 'It was an all-embrace situation down there,' he adds. 'The many genres would exist in various parts of the space: freestyle would be on the big open flat ground area near the beam at the river-side area. Slash dog style/surf would be on the big banks area. Slalom would run all the way through the whole space from the riverside to the four stairs. Street-style would be in the little banks, loading bay, bank to wall and the kicker bank in front of the four stairs.'

Rob Ashby
c. 1982

Femi Bukunola
Melon

Craig
c. 1982

BEVEL
No Parking

Cone setup for slalom
c. 1982

Shane Rouse
1984

Martin Sweeney
Slalom
c. 1982

Dieter Cole
c. 1982

John 'Bricky' Embury
c. 1982

Unknown Skateboarder
Frontside Grind
c. 1983

Jim Slater
1978

Opposite:
Davross
Frontside Boardslide

Winstan Whitter

Winstan Whitter

Fun sunny vibes down there, we would sit on the walls of the Festival Pier in the sunny sun summer time. If it was hot enough I remember people jumping into the River Thames to cool down and have a swim, dry out and have a skate.

The telephone booths were also another hangout space for us, our office! The phones served as a vital place of communication, it was the best way of knowing who was down there, or if it was wet or too busy if you were at home. Sometimes you would call and a complete stranger would call and say 'you do realize this is a public phone box' and I would reply 'yes I know' and ask them if they see any skaters there that they might be able to call over to the phone. At that time we all knew each other really well and you could locate who you needed!

Toby Shuall, Malik and Winstan Whitter

Winstan Whitter and Tom Penny

Mike Manzoori

It was on the Northern line just a few stops from Waterloo when I noticed my heart was rushing with the anticipation. Coming this far from home on a weekday solo mission, especially at that age was a bit of a bold move, but we had a half day at school and I decided to make the most of it. Saving lunch money got me the Travelcard (yes, a 4 zone card was 60p back then!) and dusk was my curfew, which really didn't leave much time to find the holy grail of London skateboarding, Southbank.

Skateboarding in the early eighties was pretty underground so the few places to skate were known by everyone, and nowhere was more popular than the smooth banks below the Queen Elizabeth Hall. It was embedded in the roots of London skateboarding from the very beginning and had established itself as the centre for skateboarding in London, not just geographically, but in spirit, so for me to take the next step in being a skateboarder I had to make the pilgrimage for myself.

As I approached the Undercroft I had a strange sense of knowing the layout of an area I had never been to just from analyzing every detail of photos in magazines of the place. Lucky for me it was a ghost town so I got to explore like a nerd for about an hour before someone else showed up to skate. I couldn't believe that this place was not made for skateboarding. Almost all of it was undercover, so the paving slab surface was spared the harsh weathering of British rain. This meant it stayed smooth and felt a bit like skating on marble. Just that alone would be enough to draw attention of skaters seeking refuge from the elements, but the layout and dimensions of the banks provided endless possibilities for skateboarding of every generation and era. It was one of the only times I have ever been there and no one else was skating. More noticeable to me at that time was that no one else was even walking about really. Unless you were going to the Royal Festival Hall or the NFT people didn't really hang around along the south side of the river back then. The transient people that used to find shelter there turned off most people from even walking through the dark Undercroft but this was not a deterrent for skateboarders who had become a permanent fixture even during the most grimy urine-stenched eras of its history.

Pretty soon my friends and I were skating there every chance we could. On the weekends we would get there as early as we could to start the day. No one was from there, we had all made a similar trek knowing that there would be somewhere to skate and people to skate with. We met so many people who came from all kinds of areas, backgrounds, and age groups. Usually this would lead naturally into adventures with new friends to new parts of London, often to skate one of the few old skate parks that remained from the seventies, or sometimes to one of the temporary ramps that popped up. For decades to follow it has been the pillar

Mike Manzoori
Frontside Boardslide

Illustration by
Jon Horner

of London's skateboarding community and gained international recognition as such. If your day skating London didn't start at Southbank it probably ended up there, and it was not unlikely you could meet people from every corner of the planet.

For several generations of skaters it served as much more then just somewhere to skate, and for a lot of us it was also a place to figure things out. Teenagers from all kinds of economic and social backgrounds who probably wouldn't necessarily have had a reason to mix were brought together on an even playing field. No one told them to be there by a certain time or even what to do once you are there, but somehow we all found the same motivation bringing us together. When I look back at what seems like infinite hours spent trying to figure out life through a skateboard I have to wonder what mischief it has saved so many of us from. It is something that will occupy a lot of time and energy for a teenager. Before skateboarding received the most recent big wave of mainstream attention started in the late nineties, most people couldn't relate to it and we were a very misunderstood minority. The idea that skateboarding can actually be a positive influence on our lost youth is still barely in its infancy today.

Over the years there have been many times when the community of skateboarders would be in a panic because news would leak of a possible redevelopment of the space we cherished so much. This would always reignite the skateboarding community to come together especially over such hallowed ground. I remember thinking these false alarms also served as very good defibrillator for the progression of skateboarding, because everyone would start trying a lot harder to use the space in different and unique ways before it was too late and gone forever. Sometimes the lights were left off to deter skaters from using the space. It was dingy in the day and completely dark once night fell which made people especially vulnerable to shady characters. Clearly having skaters around made it safer, and it's that breath of life into an otherwise mundane space that is so special.

So how does all this nostalgia relate to the big picture? How does a city benefit from space where people of all backgrounds can naturally cross paths from all over the world? A place where youths from several outcast subcultures like skateboarding, BMX, and graffiti have found a sort of harmony in refuge. Revitalising development has transformed the large area along the south side of the Thames from what was once a bit of a bleak no man's land to a place bustling with people with a lot of tourist destinations. One such tourist point of interest happens to be an unplanned, positive revision of what was essentially an "architectural dead-spot", considered by most to be a useless space in the city. Now it's no longer just skateboarders that recognize that the little area which remains of the Undercroft has become a home of British skateboarding. Now the general public is able to interact with these amazing subcultures and get to know one another. A truly progressive development of the area would be to enhance the space for skateboarding and design it in a way to include the general public. If they can't re-open the old banks blocked off in recent years, why not extend the roof out towards the river with raised walkways overlooking the skating so pedestrians walking along the Southbank can walk above, viewing the skating safely and of course adding more to skate below. Cool dreams I know, but my point is that London should proudly celebrate a unique space that has organically found and sustained a life of its own long enough to develop a history, especially one that is recognised globally.

This area has been dedicated to the arts since the 1950s, and skateboarding has been a part of it for more than half of that time since the early 1970s and in doing so established its own identity as a place that celebrates diversity through creativity and expression. More retail space is not going to make a positive change for the community especially when it comes at a cultural cost. These areas of free space where people can communicate verbally, visually and physically are like an endangered species, and must be considered precious by society and protected. They are the priceless building blocks of our culture that cannot be intentionally created or replicated.

Morbid
Frontside Wallride

Lee
Invert

Edwin Brockman
Bell Ringer

Lee
Frontside Wheelgrab

Martin Sweeney

Lee
Layback Air

1990s

Into the 1990s, the Undercroft continued to develop its reputation as an innovative and iconic skate spot. With skateboarding experiencing a resurgence in popularity towards the end of the previous decade, large crowds could once again be seen on Southbank. It seemed that the rumours of the death of skateboarding had been greatly exaggerated.

This decade saw the Southbank Centre intensifying its resistance to the activities taking place in the Undercroft. In addition to the security guards, water and stones introduced by the new owners in the 1980s, metal bars were now erected to prevent skating the banks, with the lights being turned off later in the decade to discourage night-time skating.

While designed to deter the skaters, the escalating tactics of the arts centre only served to spark their creativity, as they were forced to adapt their art to their new surroundings. Throughout the decade, the Southbank scene remained at the cutting edge of British skateboarding, while an expanding print and film media dedicated to skateboarding helped to spread the legend of Southbank to skaters across the world.

In addition to the skateboarders, a significant number of BMXers were now using the Undercroft, as well as smaller numbers of roller bladers, street artists, break dancers and other creatives. Despite their differences, the various groups were united by their love for the space, and their desire to protect and keep using it. By the close of the decade the community spirit at Southbank was stronger than ever.

Davross
Backside Footplant
2000

Lewis Ashenden
1994

Opposite:
Greg Finch
Frontside Tailslide
1998

Resistance from the Southbank Centre

Winstan Whitter

By early 1991, the Southbank Centre had had enough of us, as we expanded the spot and increased in population! They decided to get rid of us, or at least put the majority off going down there by scattering stones all over the floor and hosing down the place with water. We would actually catch them doing it because we used to go down there early on the weekends, at around 10am. We would challenge them, but it didn't really make any difference. However, we would soon find solutions! We got friendly with the cleaners and would borrow their brooms to sweep away the stones. We all took turns in this! The alternative fix for the wet floor was to pour petrol all over the wet areas and set fire to it, to burn away the water, which worked well. People would come from very far to skate Southbank – it could be Livingston in Scotland, Liverpool, Manchester, Wales, Ireland, Northampton, Oxford, Brighton – anywhere.

One rainy day in the late spring of 1991, when we arrived at Southbank, instead of being greeted by stones and water, we were surprised to find that there were 5ft tall by 8ft wide metal bars in front of all of the banks except the big banks. We were so gutted. They had been welded into the ground, so all we had left was the flat ground area and big banks. That was it: they had ruined our spot. This disheartened many of us. By this time we had all left school and had grown into teenagers exploring everything alongside skateboarding. Some gave up and went exploring, but some of us continued to skate.

Grooves dug into the concrete
1999

Opposite:
Winstan Whitter

Opposite:
Carl Shipman
Frontside 180 Kickflip
1995

After the shock of the damage done to our 'home' spot, we had to evolve quickly to keep it interesting! For a while I was bored with the new arrangement of the spot. The way it was before gave you infinite possibilities, but we were then reduced to only a few.

It was when my good old buddies like Ben Jobe, Tony Luckhurst and Femi Bukunola started ollieing over the bars that new possibilities opened up. Frontside and backside 180 ollies started happening; these then became frontside 360 ollies done only by Tony Luckhurst, who really hurt his leg doing it! Then what really pushed it was another friend from Sheffield, Carl Shipman, came down there and did a frontside 180 kick-flip over the bar – that was hot! I remember that day well: photographer Nick Hamilton took an amazing still of it at the same time as it being filmed for *411 Video Magazine*.

One fine summer's day in 1992 at Southbank, we got really frustrated with the bars. Reminiscing on life before the bars, we decided to all grab a section of the bars from one side and shake it. The bar started moving and eventually it broke away from the posts that were connected to it! We were so chuffed with the result and together threw the bar into the Thames when the tide was in. We did this to many of the bars. The Southbank Centre's reaction at first was to collect the bars out of the river and re-weld them back on to the posts in front of the banks. We kept on shaking them off for weeks until the Southbank Centre gave up. I'm sure it was because of the costs of hiring a welder every week. We got most of Southbank back, which was great fun again. The Southbank Centre went back to using the cheaper method of water and stones, then added the new device switching off the lights in summer 1993. We complained and asked why, and they responded with, 'There is a fault and we are looking into it.' This went on for about a year and we realised it was pure lies and another device to put us off skating there!

By 1996, there still were no lights on down at Southbank. It was like living in the dark ages down there! Moving shadows lurking in the darkness trying to skate at night. Lots of terrible things started happening down there. Young kids skating down there would get mugged. The only places you could see were the seven stairs and the big banks. Sometimes people would be filming for a skate video with a mini generator and lights so you could see and skate more of the space.

Good Will

The denizens of Cardboard City continued their residence at Southbank well into the 1990s. BMXer Darryl Munroe remembers one particular story involving the 'People's Princess'.

'I'm not religious anymore, and I used to hate Christmas. I used to go round Southbank and ride every Christmas after Christmas dinner and stuff with the mother and that, and basically stay away from that scene until they were done, you know? But I used to bring scraps from Christmas dinner down because I knew a couple of the guys who used to come and watch us ride all the time, and socialise and stuff. So I'd go and bring down some whisky and whatnot and scraps and just hang out with them.

'There was this woman. I can't remember exactly when it was, roughly '95 or '96 or so, maybe a little bit earlier than that. The first year – this woman – she turned up and she was all scarfed up, and she had this guy with her carrying all kinds of stuff. And I helped her distribute stuff around and she would never show her face and never say anything. But the guy would just give instructions. And the second year, same again. The same time when I'd be there they'd pull up the same time as well. But except I caught them a little bit earlier around the corner and they were having some kind of argument or whatever and I was helping to gather some of the stuff and when I came back to pick up some more stuff, she had her veil down, and I realised it was Princess Diana.'

Evolution

Neil Urwin
Nollie Hardflip

Opposite:
Jon Rattray
Frontside Bluntslide
1999

Over the decades, Southbank has developed a reputation as a workshop for UK skateboarders; a place where locals, professionals and visitors can rub shoulders and develop their skills together. Particularly from the 1990s, the Undercroft has been renowned as a training ground for rising stars in the world of street skating, who have been able to draw creative inspiration from the imperfections and limitations of the space.

Professional skater and Southbank regular Danny Brady describes how out of the ordinary surroundings can often be the stimulus to developing an individual style, having himself learnt to skate in a space even more unusual that the Undercroft. 'The whole reason I skate the way I do is because the spot I skated wasn't perfect,' he explains, 'It was a bandstand. The ledges were really round. You kind of worked with it, and because it was more difficult you had to be more creative than when you have a skatepark and you have everything perfect. So Southbank is like that. This is where I started progressing a lot, and I'd come here every day.'

As well as responding to the idiosyncratic architecture of the Undercroft, and to the new constraints increasingly imposed on them by the Southbank Centre, skaters also began to add their own touches to the space, creating new and more challenging obstacles to practice with. 'We were always trying to find new ways to skate and re-invent Southbank,' recalls Winstan Whitter, 'using jump ramps, iron girders, crash barriers, parking blocks, bread and bottle crates, plywood and picnic benches.'

For professional skaters like Nick Jensen, the Undercroft offered an environment in which to perfect specific tricks before heading out to explore the city. 'A lot of the time Southbank's like a workshop,' he explains. 'I remember before I filmed one of my last tricks for *Lost and Found*, I wanted to do a trick at the Covent Garden wheelchair ramps outside the public toilets. I measured the height of the bar, and then I went to Southbank and I laid bread crates out until I got the exact height, and I practiced doing switch ollies over it for four hours and then I went and did it. It definitely helps having somewhere like Southbank if you're a professional skateboarder, because there's not many places where you can just go to and practice without getting bothered by the public.'

The creativity that the unique space of the Undercroft inspired in skaters meant that Southbank was fast becoming recognised as a breeding ground for new talent, producing increasing numbers of professionals who would go on to achieve fame worldwide. 'So many good people have come through here over the years it's unbelievable,' observes Martin Sweeney.

For many there can be no better example of skateboarding's limitless potential for evolution than what has taken place at the Undercroft. 'Southbank has grown organically over the years,' explains Rod Broomfield, 'It embodies everything that's great about skateboarding, whether it's back in 1976 or 2013.' 'That energy and life will never stop,' adds Jensen, 'In ten years it'll be a different group of people skating a different aspect I didn't even know existed.'

Mark Channer
Fakie Heelflip the Seven
1995

Carl Shipman
Wallie Grind

Ben Jobe
180 Nosegrind

Inspiration

Increasing coverage of Southbank in magazines and videos was a huge draw for young skaters, who knew that a trip to the Undercroft might provide the opportunity to meet one of their idols. Matt Gold remembers how 'seeing The Gonz [Mark Gonzales] there skating switch blew our minds.'

Being in such close proximity to some of the biggest names in the sport also provided powerful motivation for skaters to improve their own game. 'The guys who you saw in the magazines, to actually see them in the flesh,' Chris Pullman reminisces, 'they were influences in whatever way, really big influences, a lot of us aspired to them.'

Among the many inspirational skaters of this period, Barrington Jeffrey mentions how Simon Evans 'switch 360 flipped down the stairs,' while Curtis McCann was 'doing tricks way before his time'. For south London native Lev Tanju, seeing locals like Toby Shuall, Nick Jensen and Clive Daly tearing up the Undercroft brought the once distant world of professional skateboarding much closer to home. These were 'all people that were actually from London, skating every day,' he explains, 'and it made me like London even more. Instead of idolising some guy from California, I'm watching Toby Shuall skate. It was good to get inspiration from those people and go and skate with them and be stoked on English skateboarding and London.'

One Southbank skater who stood out in particular during this period was Tom Penny. Originally from Abingdon in Oxfordshire, Penny made his first trips to the Southbank in the nineties as a teenager, before going on to make his name in the US. Many regulars from this time remember the impression Penny made, displaying a prodigious natural talent and performing tricks never before thought possible in the Undercroft. 'The stuff he used to do,' recalls Jeffrey, 'clear the seven over the edge, frontside tailslide the ledge, out forwards. No-one else has done that shit!'

Curtis McCann
1992

Mike Manzoori
Ollie over the pad
1994

Opposite:
Channon King
Blunt Fakie

Andrew Brophy
180 up 'the seven'

Jason Maldini
Ollie Japan Air
1991

Community

More than just a place to practice their particular art forms, the Undercroft provided its skaters, BMXers and other users with a feeling of community. It has been a place where bonds are made and lifelong friendships formed, offering a sense of belonging and security to its members.

'I wasn't even from here,' remembers Barrington Jeffrey, 'I had just come to London. I just came here and I meet a guy called Lewis Goodyear and he introduced me to everybody and before I knew it, I was skating down here every day and I just became friends with everybody, everybody was just cool with me and there was no attitude.'

Danny Brady remembers a similar experience finding a close community at the Undercroft when he first moved to London. 'You didn't have to call anyone,' he explains, 'You'd just come here and there'd be people here you knew, and even if it was people you didn't know it was people that were instantly your friends. That's why it's important to have a spot where you can just come – someone who's not from here can just come – and they'll have an instant community of people looking out for them. I don't think there's many other hobbies that have that. It's like a community hub. Our own little community.'

Film & Media

As well as being an innovative period in the development of skateboarding at the Undercroft, the nineties also saw new growth in the film and print media associated with the sport. A staple of British skate magazines from its earliest days, the Undercroft was now being seen and read about worldwide. A rapidly expanding market in commercial skate videos meant that Southbank and its skaters were being seen by more and more people around the world, solidifying its international reputation as the home of British skateboarding.

The emergence of Tim Leighton-Boyce's *R.A.D* in 1987 was an important catalyst in the rebirth of a vibrant British skateboarding press. Soon after, the classic *Skateboard!* magazine – which had ceased publication in the summer of 1979 – was resurrected under the editorship of Steve Kane. In 1989, the skate and BMX magazine *Freestyle* was re-launched as *Invert*, eventually becoming *Ride BMX*.

As well as providing a focal point for British magazine shoots, the Undercroft was also becoming a regular feature in popular American titles such as *Transworld* and *Thrasher*. As coverage of the spot increased throughout the 1990s, the curfew that the Southbank Centre had attempted to put in place in the previous decade became increasingly ignored, as more and more skaters flocked back to Southbank.

As a growing number of Southbank locals began to find international fame and sponsorship, the space was also becoming an increasingly popular location for skate videos. Winstan Whitter was heavily involved in the emerging skate film scene, later going on to become a successful filmmaker in his own right, directing the 2004 skate documentary *Rollin' Through the Decades*. 'The advent of skate videos first began as more skateboarders in the

UK were sponsored,' he remembers, 'Curtis McCann, Aaron Bleasdale and Mike Manzoori were London-based skaters and were a major part of the Southbank scene. They were riding for Powell Perelta and Santa Cruz, which were both major US based skate companies and through those sponsors they got lots of press coverage, especially at Southbank. People were coming from Australia, New Zealand, USA, Europe and Japan, to skate and connect with the locals down there.'

In 1991, Southbank regulars Ben Wheeler, and brothers Corin and Simon Casey put together a skate video using borrowed camcorders, under the title *Right Hard Lot*. Filmed across a number of London spots, it took the Undercroft as its main focus, opening with a shot of a sinister-looking Southbank Centre security guard patrolling the barriered-off banks. 'It featured all the local talented street skaters of the Southbank,' recalls Whitter. 'This being the only video ever made about the Southbank skate area at the time, it has become a legendary piece of skateboarding history.'

The same year saw the Blind Skateboards team in the UK to shoot what was to become one of the most influential skating films of its era. *Video Days* – directed by a young Spike Jonze and starring Mark Gonzales, Guy Mariano, Jordan Richter, Jason Lee and Rudy Johnson – was quickly recognised as a classic of the embryonic genre, providing a template that hundreds of skate films would emulate in the following decades. 'The video was almost too much to take in,' recalled *Huck* magazine's Jay Riggio in 2009. 'All I knew was that *Video Days* made me want to skate like never before. There was magic in it that to this day seems difficult to place.' 'I was a young amateur sponsored by Blind at that time,' remembers Whitter, 'and was the designated locations guy on the London section of the video. I took them straight to Southbank.'

In 1993, the bimonthly *411 Video Magazine* was set up by one of the Undercroft's regulars, Steve Douglas. 'It was Steve and Tim Leighton-Boyce who came up with the idea in a pub in Covent Garden,' remembers Whitter. *411VM* was an important step in the development of skate videos, providing skaters with a regular fix of new footage at a time when full-length videos produced by the major skate companies were still infrequent. 'Steve basically gave us one video camera for the whole of the UK,' remembers Whitter, and we passed it around all the scenes and skate spots for about a year. Southbank was one of the first stops. This is where we all learned how to film each other skateboarding, and really put Southbank on the map with the first retrospective guide to London.'

Mark Channer
Frontside Boardslide
1999

Opposite:
Toby Shaull
Switch Heelflip

BMX

As well as the developing styles of skateboarding taking place at the Undercroft during the 1990s, the BMX scene was also becoming more established. While skating remained the dominant activity associated with the space, Winstan Whitter recalls that 'there was a big BMX scene there, and we always shared the space and knew each other. The BMXers would use the riverside flat ground area, from the two stairs to the top of the big banks.'

Darryl Munroe has been BMXing at the Southbank for more than 20 years. He was born in London, but moved to Jamaica as a small child, only returning to the UK at the age of 22. He made his first visit to the Undercroft in the early nineties.

'I actually stumbled upon it,' he recalls, 'I was just walking over the river, and starting going to the end where there was absolutely nobody and nothing at all. I could see some concrete banks from there and I thought to myself, "That's going to be good." I walked over and I could hear clack, clack, clack and some things going on and I thought, "Those are definitely skateboarders." Then I saw a BMXer carve in and out, so I started rushing over and then I got there and, just, that was it. I stopped there the whole day. I even forgot where to go home afterwards, and some of the guys from there showed me how to get back to Clapham Junction, and we became friends ever since.'

For the BMX community, Munroe explains, Southbank is seen as 'the iconic spot', the home of the sport in London and in the UK. Just as the unique architecture of the Undercroft has stimulated creative responses from skaters over the decades, BMXers have found that the space, while not designed for riding, provides a unique experience that is difficult to replicate elsewhere, and which forces riders to adapt and develop their skills.

'You know how sudden Southbank's banks are. If you're not used to the timing of that, the rhythm of it can pull you down – pull you apart. And that's the challenge of it so it's important in that way.'

Whether you're an experienced rider or just a beginner, explains Munroe, 'It's still a challenge regardless.' The appeal of the Undercroft is that it is both 'a difficult street spot' for the experienced BMXer, and at the same time, 'for beginners and guys who don't always ride that much, it's a good place to go because it pushes you as well.'

Finally, he adds, 'It's just a beautiful spot to be at as well because it's close to the river.'

KOD•AK
51
KOD•AK TX 6043
TX 9

Interview: Ben Jobe

What is your name?

Andrew Makkonen, aka Ben Jobe.

And where are you from?

Peckham.

What do you do for a living?

Yoga, flute, meditation, peace, love and harmony growth.

What do you do at Southbank?

All the above, plus skateboard. Oh, also much more as expression is fun there.

When did you first visit Southbank and what did you make of it?

When I was 15 and it was fun.

Why is it important to you today?

It is still fun even though half of it is gone.

How does what you do at Southbank fit into your life in outside Southbank?

Balance is everything.

What is the most memorable experience you have had at Southbank?

Too many and the universe is genius and loves me so much I don't feel like boasting here.

Have you got any stories about Southbank that you'd like to share?

I went to a Southbank Centre meeting and the woman who worked for them said, "I know it is the mecca for skateboarding". Now I think it used to be, before they destroyed half of it for what I consider to be rubbish in comparison.

How would you feel if the space was redeveloped

Meditate and/or pray for enough change to make this world even better than it is for all our futures shared.

Ben Jobe
Fakie Nosegrind
2002

Ben Jobe
Backside Nosegrind
2002

Opposite:
Ben Jobe
Ollie out to Noseslide

Andrew Brophy
Ollie the rubble

2000s

The popularity of skateboarding rose to an all-time high in the early 2000s, with the success of *Tony Hawk's Pro Skater*, a game that inspired millions to pick up skateboards and brought many new, young faces to the Undercroft. In the fourth incarnation of Tony Hawk's game, Southbank was chosen as the main skate spot in London due to its iconic status as the birthplace of British skateboarding.

The increased popularity of skateboarding at this time gave major British skate companies a wider customer base, and many Southbank skaters who rode for London-based brands such as Blueprint, Heroin and Landscape Skateboards became famous worldwide, with their footage at the Undercroft playing an integral part in their success. Dan Magee's iconic skate video *Lost and Found*, released in 2005, propelled the London skate scene into the forefront of global skate media. A series of notable Southbank skate alumni featured in the video including Nick Jensen, Danny Brady, Chewy Cannon, Vaughan Baker and Neil Smith.

As well as looking forward to a bright future, skaters also began to develop an interest in their own past. In volumes ranging from skater-turned-academic Iain Borden's scholarly *Skateboarding, Space and the City* (2001) to Jocko Weyland's vibrant personal memoir of the American skate subculture, *The Answer is Never* (2002), different writers began to document the history of skateboarding, and the sport that for so long had been an 'underground' phenomenon began to be brought to the attention of the wider public.

Winstan Whitter's documentary *Rollin' Through the Decades*, released in 2004, told the story of British skateboarding from its 1970s origins to its present heyday, with one spot standing out as an obvious focus. 'The Southbank area was always going to be the backbone of the story,' recalls Winstan. *Rollin' Through the Decades* documented the role of the Undercroft in the development of modern skateboarding and helped a new generation of skaters enthused by contemporary fashions and video games to understand the significance of what had come before.

While skateboarding and its history were catching the imagination of millions of people around the world, however, and fast penetrating the consciousness of mainstream media, no such enthusiasm was to be found from the Undercroft's owners. The first decade of the new millennium saw decades-old tensions between the skateboarders and the Southbank Centre intensify to an unprecedented degree. From 2004–05, the Undercroft was dramatically reduced in size, as large sections were requisitioned for use as 'temporary' storage or office space during the refurbishment of the Festival Hall, leaving a space barely one third of its original size.

Collaboration with skateboarding art collective The Side Effects of Urethane to install a series of skateable sculptures in the Undercroft briefly seemed to offer the Southbank Centre a chance at reconciliation, but by the time the Festival Hall reopened in 2007 – and the Southbank Centre's promises to restore the 'little banks' remained unfulfilled – any residual trust among the Undercroft community had well and truly evaporated. Rumours began to spread that the space which had been home to British skateboarding and urban arts for over three decades was now at risk of total closure.

The later years of the decade saw the Undercroft community organise itself into an effective campaign group in an attempt to secure the future of its beloved space. A film documenting the importance of Southbank was produced to get the message out, while a petition delivered to Downing Street put the fate of the Undercroft on the national political agenda. Embarrassed by the swell of public opinion in favour of the skateboarders, the Southbank Centre reassured the Undercroft community that there were no plans for closure, and by the end of the decade, both sides were committed to developing a positive working relationship.

In spite of the reduction of the space, for the first time in its history, it felt as if the Undercroft had found a harmony with its surroundings. The public interest in skateboarding gripped people like never before. Furthermore, after years of conflict, it seemed that, by the end of the decade, the Southbank Centre had embraced the skate community, and had permitted them to take up permanent residence in the Undercroft.

The End of the Little Banks

From its early uses as a skating location, many skaters recollect how they used the entirety of the Southbank. The area now known as the Undercroft is only the last remaining part of the much larger area used by the early pioneers, which included the Shell Centre podium beside County Hall, the 'Birdshit Banks' beneath Hungerford Bridge, and often sections of the riverside Queen's Walk. The Undercroft itself originally stretched the whole way beneath the Queen Elizabeth Hall and its walkways, allowing a clear view from the river walk to the road behind.

The hostility of the Southbank Centre towards skaters, involving the installation of anti-skateboarding devices, the turning out of lights and other deliberate attempts to dissuade skaters from using the area, culminated in 2004–05 in the closing off of the famous 'little banks'. The effect of the closure was to drive some of the regular skaters away forever and cause a major transformation of the Undercroft.

Throughout the decades, users of the space have been baffled by the owners' antagonism towards skateboarders. For Toby Shuall the changes to the overall site left an irreparable mark on the area. 'Being older it's weird,' he muses 'because it's not the place where I grew up. I coined this phrase: the world I'm from is dead. It's quite bleak but unfortunately it's true. As far as the place that I grew up skateboarding with – I don't know what my generation is or whatever – it's kind of gone. That place is kind of like a theme park.'

In the early 2000s, the Southbank and surrounding area by the Shell Centre was considered the hub of London skating, supported by the Cide skate shop from 2002, which played a pivotal role in contributing to the survival of the space by putting in obstacles, holding competitions and lobbying against closure. Jin Shimizu recollects the atmosphere at the time: 'There was a very DIY feel about the place back then, it was a lot bigger and the blocks weren't there – people would just find things lying around like cones or pieces of wood and that would become the

session.' Yet these days were numbered, as Greg Finch from Cide remembers: 'Unfortunately the Shell Centre spot got closed for some redevelopment reason. We had a small hand in delaying the Southbank redevelopment, but not without a concession, which meant the end of the little banks. This took quite a lot away from the original layout of the skateable Southbank, in my opinion.'

After years of tension between skaters and the Southbank Centre, Winstan Whitter recollects how the process of reduction began: 'During this time in 2004, the Southbank Centre had started major works on the Royal Festival Hall as part of its refurbishment. They needed storage space so they commandeered half our skate spot. They started fencing off the little banks, temporary offices had moved in – before you knew it they were knocking away all of the little banks and loading bays. Over 50% of the space got hoarded off for Festival Hall storage. At this time we had no idea what was going on even though we were asking the builders and security.'

Panoramic view of the little banks

Hoarding and development
of the Little Banks
2000–2005

For many skaters it was the closure of the little banks that heralded the most deadly blow to skateboarding at the site. Southbank Sam remembers how he felt: 'Devastated, devastating, that's all I can say, devastating, I was gutted, those little banks were the life and soul. The big banks were good as well but they were so underused.' Daniel Vitalsound also ponders on the 'gradual reduction of the available space, getting shrunk ever smaller as the commercial development took hold to either side, swallowing up the small banks as well as "birdshit banks" down the path.'

Yet within these laments are kernels of positivity, as the creative energy of the Southbank skateboarders was challenged once again by the restrictions placed on their environment. 'Out of adversity comes creativity,' Vitalsound continues 'and thanks to the placement of a few concrete ledges and blocks, some hacksaw work on the fences, and an upturn in skating's mainstream popularity, the Southbank stays busy and still new tricks are being done on a daily basis.' Nick Jensen also sees the possibilities within the challenges: 'Even though it's smaller, it's got different elements to it. The level of progress is insane. People from the seventies would not believe it. I think the whole progression thing is hard to talk about because obviously people from the seventies would be tripping if they saw it now.'

Dennis Durrant
Kickflip BS Noseblunt
2006

Opposite:
Dan Callow

Moving Units

In the same year as it was reduced in size, the Undercroft underwent another transformation at the hands of critically acclaimed skateboarding art collective The Side Effects of Urethane, headed by Toby Shuall and Rich 'Badger' Holland. The architecture and sculpture project, entitled Moving Units, involved the installation of a series of new ledges and blocks in the Undercroft that quickly became popular with the locals.

Shortly after completing a successful skate architecture project at PlayStation skate park in 2004, The Side Effects of Urethane team brought their unique combination of skateboarding, art, philosophy, design and architecture to Southbank, with the creation of five new skateable concrete sculptures. Toby Shuall, Rich Holland and other skaters used a wheeled loading dock to hoist the new ledges out of the van and into the Undercroft. There was a celebratory jam to welcome the installation and the skaters were happy to see new skate blocks in the Undercroft that they could test new tricks on.

13
CLEAR

1B

The first instalments by the group included an uphill 'cheese wedge' block, which could be used in multiple ways: as a manual pad, a grinding block, and a kicker. There was also a ledge with two levels, giving it a greater range of difficulty. These blocks would later be replaced by two other stages of the Moving Units project, with each ledge that was installed in the space different to the ones that had been there previously. This ethos suited the transient nature of the spot, with just enough time for skaters to learn and hone their skills on a new obstacle before it was replaced by something different.

Coming at a time when increasing encroachment from the Southbank Centre seemed to put the future of the space in jeopardy, the skater-led project was welcomed by Undercroft users and helped to fuel a new wave of enthusiasm and creativity at Southbank.

Since the inception of the Moving Units project, the Undercroft has seen an influx of smooth and technical ledge skating due to the inclusion of these blocks, which have become a staple of the Undercroft's environment. Although found material such as planters, cones and discarded bits of sheet metal are still used, the blocks have brought a new dimension to the spot, with modern ledge skating added to Undercroft skaters' ever-growing repertoire.

Chris Oliver
Noseblunt Slide
2005

Mike Sutcliffe
Frontside 360
2005

Danny Barnet
Frontside Smith Backside 180 out
2005

Broken Promises

It seemed as if the Moving Units project had inaugurated a shift towards a more positive relationship between the users of the Undercroft and the Southbank Centre. The graffitied mural that formed the backdrop to the exhibition marked the start of a period that would see the Southbank Centre relax their attitude to street art, seeing the Undercroft become one of the most dynamic and iconic legal graffiti spots in the capital. At the same time, Southbank Centre installed improved lighting and repaired cracked pavements to help facilitate skateboarding.

Speaking of the Moving Units sculptures, Southbank Centre chief executive Michael Lynch – who claimed to have skateboarded himself as a boy growing up in Australia – put on record his intention to 'give access to what seems to be almost an ancestral ground for skateboarders,' and to begin a new policy of 'talking rather than fighting' with the Undercroft users. 'A lot of people enjoy watching the skateboarders and the tricks they perform,' added commercial director Mike McCart, 'They have found a very good use for a space we had not been able to find a use for, and we are very happy for them to use that location.'

Over the next year, however, Undercroft users saw the space available for skating get smaller and smaller. As the Festival Hall was closed to the public to allow refurbishment work to take place, more of the Undercroft was annexed for office use, with temporary fences replaced by more permanent looking walls. Where once it had been possible to skate the whole way beneath the Queen Elizabeth Hall, by the summer of 2005 skaters were restricted to a small area on the riverfront, with close to two thirds of the original space now inaccessible.

Andrew Brophy
Noseblunt

Lewis Marnell
Frontside 180 Heelflip

In response to protests from outraged skateboarders and other users of the Undercroft, none of whom had been consulted before the changes were made, the Southbank Centre issued a statement, reassuring them that the closure was only temporary, and that 'as much of the Undercroft space as possible' would be released when the Festival Hall was reopened.

By summer 2007 however, with the Festival Hall reopened amid much ceremony, it was looking increasingly like the 'temporary' reductions to the Undercroft were there to stay. Despite new offices opening alongside Hungerford Bridge, there was no indication that the little banks would be reopened as promised. With the success of the new shops and restaurants which had appeared beneath the Festival Hall (complete with built-in anti-skate devices) helping to pay for the renovation bill, rumours began to circulate that the skate area would soon be going the same way, with the Southbank Centre seeking to cash in on the Undercroft's prominent riverside location.

While Southbank Centre management claimed that they had no intentions to redevelop the site, the skaters had learned by now not to take them at their word. Under the leadership of Toby Shuall and Winstan Whitter, the director of the successful skate documentary *Rollin' Though the Decades*, the skaters got organised. In early 2008, as Mayor Ken Livingstone declared his view that skateboarding should feature in the forthcoming London Olympic Games, a petition to save the Undercroft attracting over 4,000 signatures was delivered to the office of Prime Minister Gordon Brown, and received a positive response. 'Any activity that engages and develops young people can have a very positive impact on society,' read the Downing Street statement, 'and the skateboarding community that has grown up around the Undercroft has brought together people from various backgrounds, created a vibrant public space and added real value to the lives of many young people.'

In February 2008, as Winstan and Toby's film, *Save Southbank,* premiered at the Prince Charles Cinema, the Southbank Centre was forced to issue a statement confirming that there were no plans to redevelop the site in the immediate future, and that skateboarders were regarded 'as an important part of the creative community.'

The Undercroft, at least for the time being, was safe.

Nick 'Zorlac' Orechio
FS Wallride Grab Off
1982–83

Crossfire Skate Jams

Zac Leeks

Adam Howe takes cash on
the infamous seven set

I found myself at age 14 back in 1987 taking a train to Waterloo to visit the Southbank for the first time with a bunch of friends from school. Following a quick stop at the Casey Jones burger joint and a chase from the guards across the smooth marble floor, we reached the Shell Centre steps for a session and then finally on to the Undercroft's cold concrete slabs.

I can clearly remember the echo of wood cracking against the concrete floor as we arrived; it seemed haunting, yet so very satisfying. This haunting feeling was derived from the hazy sunlight that shone between the Thames and the Undercroft floor as we sat watching everyone skate sat on the wooden ledge. This sight and sound was to be a familiar occurrence as it was that very day I conquered my very first kick turn on the small banks. Little did I know at that point in time that this moment that would change my life, forever.

The liberation from that one trip gave me so much confidence and opened up a world I really had no idea about. As a result, my fascination for skateboarding grew rapidly. Magazines were purchased, other skateboarders were identified and Southbank visits then became weekly which allowed me to meet many like-minded people, but also taught me of the dangers that came with cruising around London. Tramps would expose themselves on those visits; other kids would try and mug you for your board, watch and cash. It was pot luck whether you returned home with your pride intact but all of these fears and thrills where served up at Southbank in the 80s and those experiences made us what we are today. It's funny looking back at that scene now and remembering that our main worry wasn't the fear of being stabbed by muggers – kingpins were hard to find around those parts in the 80s, so if you broke one of those on your trucks, you had a long journey ahead of you to Slam City Skates!

I grew up in the same town as Curtis McCann in Sutton, Surrey and although he was younger, he took to that place like a duck to water and soon became a local hero and a sponsored UK skateboarder. Many others from our area followed suit and took their creativity to new levels including my good friend who is now known as the artist D*Face. We all found ourselves skating through the chaos served up from the Smell of Death events and other regular gatherings. The Wednesday night sessions at Southbank were incredible. The very best skaters would always be there sessioning the banks, 'the seven', the wall and creating energy that you will never find anywhere else.

All of this and everything in between was a catalyst for me starting Crossfire in 2001. The London skate scene didn't have many skate events on offer, so I decided to design a paper zine which led to various parties, jams and the online magazine that you can still see at caughtinthecrossfire.com today. It was all down to congregating with creative people and enjoying life at Southbank.

In 2005, we decided to throw a Seven-Set Jam event there. It was my way of giving the spot something back and was very much inspired by Steve Wilshere's legendary Smell of Death events. Danny Brady took the honours with a fakie double flip, a fakie frontside flip, double flip and backside double flip. Neil Smith graced the place with a backside nollie heelflip, nollie bigspin heelflip, and switch frontside bigspin heelflip. James Gardner's switch frontside 360 also took cash on the day. It was totally packed down there. All we had was a crappy stereo and a loudspeaker. Smiffy unfortunately went home in an ambulance after giving everything.

In 2006, I was involved in the CIDE shop behind the Southbank and Rich 'Badger' Holland, Sam Griffin and I decided to open up a new line down there in preparation for another Seven-Set event. Badger had already delivered a concrete cheese block to skate amongst other concrete delights, but we wanted to concrete over the cobbles to form a new manny pad for everyone to skate. We carried concrete mix and water bottles in there about midnight, and walked out of there covered in dust as the quick dry cement did its thing. Looking back, it served the event well, but I wish we had completed the entire area rather than half of it but it was all we could carry!

Over 500 people filled the Southbank for that event. It was quite overwhelming. At 2.30pm before we kicked off the jam we held a minute's silence dedicated to Matt McMullen who had sadly passed. He was a Southbank and Stockwell regular for years and will never be forgotten. It's incredible to think of all of the characters who have graced this place. The spot is like a magnet that draws in strange characters and bonds everyone together.

Seth Curtis
Cheese block Wallie 5-0

Opposite:
Vaughan Baker bluntstall flip fakie's the cheese block

Chris Ault mid-frontside flip on 'the seven'

Opposite:
Louie Barletta nosepicks into the big banks.

Ben Grove backtail shuvit on the ledge with a broken deck

John Warwicker
Legendary balls-out tre-flip

Lucien Clarke
Bigspin 'the seven'

Louie Barletta was in town from the US on that day and brought a wallie lipslide on the cheese block before taking a front blunt flip into the big banks. That was a defining moment. The place was buzzing. Australian ripper Josh Roullion took a backside tail stall to bigspin into the bank and frontside nosegrind revert that also got props. Chris Oliver then ollied the entire cobbled area making everyone scream in delight before Adam Howe blew 'the seven' with a switch 360 shuvit. What a day.

In 2007, we threw the last of these annual events. This time with guests from Darkstar Skateboards in attendance. Terell Robinson, Gailea Momolou, Marley and Adam Dyet were all present with Thrasher photographer Rhino. Over 600 people saw the police turn up to ask what the hell we were doing before Dyet grabbed cash with a nollie cab heelflip down 'the seven' and a perfect kickflip frontside noseslide on the ledge. A local chav tried to bum rush the free product toss and was maimed by everyone. Even a London skater called John Warwicker tried tre-flipping the stairs naked! Good times were had!

I cannot tell you how much fun it was to be present as these events, let alone to have hosted them. Another little slice of history was etched into those banks each time we all congregated there. Thank you if you are reading this and were there to make them so much fun, as without you, they would have been nothing.

Long Live Southbank and the great people and memories that have made it so legendary.

Adam Dyet
Fakie flip

Opposite:
Chris Oliver's straight ollie over the freshly laid manny pad

The product toss

PWBC

Palace Wayward Boys Choir

The Palace Wayward Boys Choir or PWBC is a well-known crew of skaters who lived in Brixton and later Waterloo in the early 2000s. The name comes from the original house they lived in together, which they dubbed 'The Palace'. Since its creation, the PWBC has grown in size and fame as the quintessential London skate crew.

The PWBC has transformed since its humble origins and many of the original members are now seasoned professional skate-boarders and well-respected artists in their own right. In 2009, Lev Tanju used his knowledge of skateboarding and an archive of skate footage to create a popular topical online skateboarding news show, dubbed *Global Skateboarding News*. After the show ended, Tanju announced his new company, Palace Skateboards, which had stalwart PWBC crew members, Lucien Clarke, Olly Todd and Charlie Young and later Rory Milanes and Chewy Cannon on its official team. Palace Skateboards became very popular very quickly, due to its eclectic team, original skate videos and its sought-after high quality clothing, and in its first year, this was recognised by the skate community when it won the 2010 Brand of the Year award at the Bright Tradeshow in Berlin.

The first PWBC skate videos were filmed on skaters' camera phones, giving the footage a gritty audio and visual aesthetic, which was unique compared to other videos available in skate-boarding media. To add to this, the PWBC skaters skated British spots like Southbank in a fast and loose way, which emanated a sense of raw, organic, very British skateboarding. This grittiness was embedded in the Palace Skateboards brand. At a time when the majority of skate productions were being produced on high definition cameras, Tanju bought an old VHS camera and shot all of the Palace videos with it. The lo-fi nature of their skate videos and the PWBC skateboarders' authenticity as real street skaters and not energy-drink sponsored skate park superstars caught the attention of the skate world. Nowadays the return of VHS filming and lo-fi production is more commonplace, but most recognise Palace as pioneers in presenting modern skating in this way.

Lev Tanju

Opposite:
Stu Hammond
2013

Over the years the PWBC has grown, however the core members of the PWBC still active today are Levant Tanju, Andrew Brophy, Billy Bernard Baxter, Chewy Cannon, Stuart Hammond, Rory Milanes, Lucien Clarke, Danny Brady, Nick Jensen, Benny Fairfax, Joey Pressey, Snowy, Charlie Young, Oliver Todd, Oliver Mackintosh, Rum and Coke, James Edson, Rob Mathieson, Gabriel Pluckrose, Happy Ben and Karim Bhaktaoui.

Palace Skateboards' varied and high-quality range of clothing became an internationally popular streetwear brand. Notable wearers of Palace clothing include, R&B superstar Rhianna, rappers Rick Ross and A$AP Rocky and London-based music artist Florence Welch (Florence and the Machine).

The PWBC was started as a way for a group of friends to join together in the pursuit of raw street skating. Tanju felt there was a lack of authenticity and rawness in skating and that his friends didn't have adequate sponsors so he started Palace as a way to promote the things that he valued in skateboarding that he felt the current generation had forgotten.

The PWBC has risen organically out of the community of skateboarders at the Southbank. Trends have come and gone but they have remained true to the principles they believe in, an ethos that they have all learned from their time skating the Undercroft and being an integral part of its community.

Lev Illustration by
Rob Mathieson

Opposite:
Lev Tanju

Interview: Wig Worland

When did you first start taking photographs?

I started working as a photographer's assistant in the late 1980s and also at the same time I was a skateboarder so eventually, I put the two together. Not immediately, but after a year or two, when I thought I knew enough about photography. I learnt photography in a studio, so I learnt about lighting, and I always wanted to be able to build a studio in the street and that is what I am synonymous with in the skateboard photography world.

How did you get interested in photography in the first place?

Probably at school, and then I managed to get a job as a photographer's assistant straight out of school. I was fairly lucky that I just fell into assisting a photographer. He was a very good commercial photographer who really knew what he was doing so I learnt very quickly. He expected a lot from me.

Why do you think it's important to take photos?

Life's so transitory isn't it? I think Larry Clark, the guy who directed *Kids* said to a friend of mine something like, 'you've got to shoot the people you have around you, now', don't question why, just do it and then in years to come, you'll be able to look back on that historical moment and it'll be a wonderful thing. Just take pictures kids, get out there and do it! You just never know what is going to be important or inspirational to others.

Chris Pulman
Frontside No-Comply 'the seven'
2000

When was the first time you took note of skateboard photography?

Probably in the mid-eighties. Specifically Spike Jonze's work probably. That now very well known film director was working for a magazine called *Club Home Boy* or *Freestylin'* back in the mid-eighties so that's when I first noticed it. In England, there was a magazine called *BMX Action Bike* which slowly turned, over a number of issues, into *R.A.D* magazine. Tim Leighton-Boyce was responsible for that and changed our lives with his images, so that was the British influence as well.

While you were growing up, were there any images that impacted you or your style of photography outside of skateboarding?

Andreas Gursky, Trent Parke, Martin Parr. I loved all the *NME* photographers as well in it's heyday, people like Derek Ridgers, Steve Pyke and Kevin Cummins. I don't know whether you can see the influence in my work but that was what I was into. Also the New British Colour photography movement with people like Paul Graham, though I guess you could put Martin Parr in there as well. With the advent of *Sidewalk* magazine, I think I consciously looked for a way to express the Britishness of the very different UK skate scene. I didn't want it to look just like all the American stuff that we were seeing at the time. I guess people will judge for themselves if we succeeded.

What were your initial experiences of the Southbank Undercroft? When did you first go there?

I would've gone there first as a skateboarder. It was this great big, quite foreboding space that you'd go to on a Wednesday night starting in the mid-eighties and it was amazing. A huge, open space, free, in the middle of the city. It was incredible. I didn't live in London then so I didn't go there that often, I wasn't there every week, but when we did go there it was great.

Would you say that the photography that you've done at Southbank has had an effect on your career as a photographer?

It suited my style, I suppose, because I wanted to come along and I wanted to set up a studio in the street, so Southbank was able to give me was a space to do that. There was a period when they didn't want you to be there so they'd throw stones on the ground etc., but after that, they were a bit more welcoming and certainly when I started getting a bit more involved in the skateboard world and working for a skateboard magazine, you could go down there and set up lights and set up the sort of studio I wanted to set up and shoot all day and no one would bother you, whereas in other areas of the city, we'd be chased off. Setting up a studio, effectively, with lights, outside a large merchant bank in the City probably wouldn't last that long so yes, I was able to practice that technique in that space.

Who were the most influential skaters at Southbank at the time you did most of your photography?

Ben Jobe. That's it. The end. Ben Jobe was really the most exciting, incredible talent there. Everyone else visited, of course, but he virtually lived there and he was magic in that space. All the Americans would turn up and they'd do incredible things but Ben Jobe is synonymous with that space.

What is your favourite photo that you shot at Southbank?

Ben Jobe's backside tail slide with all the locals and others in the background, probably.

Are there any new photographers whose photos of Southbank inspire you?

There have been so many. People like Dom Marley, Oli Barton and Sam Ashley all took that setting up a studio in the street thing and took it further and have done it better and have been able to use more modern technology as well. Because it's so dark underneath the Undercroft, it needs lighting and they've all done it much better than me. Tim Leighton-Boyce likes to do his photography down, but of course, it was hugely influential and brilliant in its era.

Ben Jobe
Backside Tailslide
1996

Snowy
Backside Nollie Flip
2002

What is unique about Southbank in terms of photography?

It is really bloody dark. In the film days, it was impossible to photograph down there without bringing extra lighting in. Now, of course, you can just turn your camera up to ridiculous ISO, but actually I'm sure it all looks really grey still. It is really grey, with those paving slabs. The colour of the original concrete always made me think I might as well be in there shooting black and white. Eventually, some skateboarders like Mat Fowler and Mike Manzoori would realise this and started to wear brightly coloured T shirts. The contrast against the grey was really striking so certain people really got that. But, essentially, you might as well have been shooting in black and white. Maybe that's the draw of the place, those paving slabs, they look so rugged and so horrible in pictures but when you're rolling up to the seven, it is beautifully smooth.

Why is Southbank important to you?

I suppose it's been part of my life for quite a long time, I did have some amazing experiences there actually skateboarding probably in the mid 1980s when I was very young and it made me, for the first time probably, think that skateboarding was an incredibly important activity. It felt like, because the space was so big, it felt as important as something like surfing. It was just one of those amazing childhood experiences. I can't quite put it into words.

Why is Southbank important to London?

What an incredible thing that free space is available right in the centre of London, and 20 years ago nobody cared about the entire Southbank, never mind the Southbank Centre. It was a complete no man's land so it felt like a much more free place to be.

Did you ever see Tom Penny skate there?

I did. He is this British legend that is/was incredibly talented. He never quite fulfilled his potential totally, though some people might argue with me about that in terms of the specifics of it. He's a sort of Jim Morrison type character even though he's still alive. He's just a naturally talented brilliant skateboarder who was always slightly removed from the scene. People talk about this one night where he was getting people to call out tricks to him and he would do them but of course all these tricks that he was doing, one after the other, down the seven had all been done before and of course, he didn't want me to shoot him doing 'that trick again' down there so we don't have that many pictures of Tom there because he would ask us not to shoot him, which is a bit of a pity really. But I was there that night and it was amazing. But, very much like with Ben Jobe, you can't make it happen. It either happens or it doesn't with Tom. You can't orchestrate a shoot. You have to hang about with him and if the magic works, that's brilliant, if not, try another day.

What is it like shooting Ben Jobe?

Similarly, you had to hang about and wait for it all to happen and when it would it would be brilliant. Actually, I got to know Ben a little bit better than that and I was getting him into it and he got a bit more receptive to being photographed. It was in the early 2000s. He had definitely earned it and maybe he was feeling a bit like 'it's now or never', so that was a good thing to do.

Ben's 180 nosegrind down the hubba was a real turning point in terms of progression, how did that come about?

I'd say actually Ben Jobe would've just done that trick or had a go at it at least once a week back then. I just happened to be there in the right place at the right time when the magic happened.

Was it the same with the Ben Jobe back tail shot? He's pre-lock and it looks so intense. Did you know it would be such an epic shot?

There are other frames on the film where he's 'locked', I could have chosen one of those, but I was slightly more maverick back then. Skateboarding media is, in some ways, quite conservative and it has an attitude of 'we've got to represent this in this way' and maybe that was an early attempt at representing something in a slightly different way because, for me, that particular shot is a bit of an iconic moment. All the people in the background, including Tom Penny, and for me it's more pregnant, it's the 'what's going to happen' that's the point. That's why I chose that particular frame rather than choosing one of the more obvious frames on the roll.

Benny Fairfax
Backside Lipslide
2000

Opposite:
Channon King
50-50 in the pier
1998

Benny Fairfax's back lipside with all the kids holding the rail is an amazing shot. You feel a real sense of community. What's the story behind that photo?

It really does look like that I suppose, doesn't it? Benny was down there a lot and lived very nearby at the time so he was skating there all the time. He's a very big name in skateboarding now and certainly at that moment it was obvious that he was going to be. He is obviously very talented. So I guess he knew everybody so it was Benny who orchestrated that. And the kid at the front who is holding the barrier, that's a real amount of trust isn't it? A magic moment. That's the type of thing that happens in that space at the Southbank. You're there and things come together. I think he had done that before though, with the kids holding the barrier without a photographer down there so he knew he could definitely do it. That's my impression of it anyway.

The photo of Channon King's 50-50 on the access ramp rail is ridiculous. How did that come about?

Channon had done it and was raving on about it and nobody could quite believe it because that thing is tidal, it goes up and down and at certain times of the day you can't do it because it's too flat, and at certain times of the day you can't do it because it's too steep. So we kept going back there when it wasn't quite right. Then right time, right place again.

Are there any great tricks that remain undocumented that you weren't able to shoot?

Yes, I'm sure there are lots. I am absolutely convinced I saw Ben Jobe do a barefoot half cab over the barriers for instance. That remains undocumented, definitely. It's the kind of late night Ben Jobe moment that happens when no-one's got a camera out.

Female Skaters of Southbank

Women have always represented a minority within the skate scene. In their very marginality, however, they have perhaps been able to best embody what skateboarding has always been about: an alternative mode of creative expression through which young people can break free of dominant social codes.

It is a sad truth that even within a subculture that has been defined by its disregard for authority and for society's norms, old-fashioned gender discrimination has far too often gone unchallenged. The last few years have seen a lot of progress made, with groups such as the Girls Skate Network in the US and the Boardettes in the UK working to improve the position of women within the sport. Even today however, women in skateboarding often find themselves defined more by their gender than their ability, while a Google search for 'female skateboarders' takes you first of all to a list of the 'The 10 Sexiest'.

While in many places, 'skating like a girl' is still considered an insult, for the inclusive community of the Undercroft, divisions such as gender – as well as those of colour, nationality and social background – have always been secondary to the bonds of mutual interest and respect that have held the space together. For decades, female skaters from around the world have been drawn to the Southbank for the much the same reasons as men – because of its history, prestige and iconic status within the skateboarding scene – safe in the knowledge that they will be able to participate on an equal footing.

Women have been rolling around the Undercroft alongside their male counterparts for just as many years, each with their own story to tell about their experiences there. Here are just a few.

Caroline Dynibil
2012

Jenna Selby, 34, Hertfordshire:

Back in the late nineties I met a girl called Dee Sansom at a club in London. We became good friends and she persuaded me to buy a board. As she lived in Burnham and I was in Herts we used to arrange to meet every Sunday down at Shell Centre (round the back of Southbank). We'd skate the steps there for a while before heading off into town. Later on in the evening we'd head back to Southbank when it would be a bit quieter and roll around the banks until late. I guess one of my most memorable times down there was the time Dee and I thought it was a good idea to skate-in the New Years, I think it was 1998–9. For the first hour it was fun, then it kind of dawned on us just how cold it would be to stay in the spot for 5 hours. From what I remember we did stick it out due to sheer stubbornness more than enjoyment. And we were on a train quick smart at 12.05 trying to de-thaw!

In 2005 I set up a female skate team called Rogue Skateboards (which at the time comprised of Lucy Adams, Maria Falbo, Sadie Hollins, Laura Goh and myself). There was no question about location for our very first team skate, it had to be Southbank. Through skating the Undercroft, either with the team or with other friends, over the years I have met many other girls who've inspired me to keep on doing what I'm doing.

A found space such as this can never be recreated. Those who try are blind to the very essence of what skating is about, and that this is one of the few places that really represents what skateboarding means. With the shift in attitude from councils to get more skaters into parks and off the streets, it is perhaps more important now than ever before to realise the importance of Southbank and why it needs to be preserved.

Heidi Blum, 30, Surrey:

I came to London from Austria to study when I was 18. Southbank was not only my favourite skate spot but also a place where I met amazing people. I spent many, many nights skating at the Southbank with one or two friends. The beauty of the river at night and the fun we had skating the banks has left memories and emotions that definitely influenced my decision to make London home. There was always a friendly vibe and I always thought the skaters at the Undercroft formed an integral part of the tourist attraction that is the Southbank.

Southbank has played an important part in the history of skateboarding and since skateboarders form an ever-growing part of the London community, it is of historic relevance for the city itself. The enjoyment tourists and passers-by seem to get out of watching the skateboarders also suggests that losing it would take away some of the areas charm.

Sadie Hollins
2009

Sadie Hollins, 26, Enfield

Southbank was one of the really famous spots growing up that was on all of the skate vids and mags that everyone spoke about – 'so and so did this trick down "the seven"'. It was almost like a bit of a pilgrimage for all the guys I used to skate with and we would try and go as many Sundays as we could.

I found Southbank – a bit like marmite – for my friends you either loved it or hated it but I absolutely loved skating there. Seeing so many good skaters really motivated me to learn and try new tricks. I always felt that I had improved after skating there.

It was also amazing that people from all over the world would come to skate Southbank and it really brought people together – skaters and non-skaters alike – and I still remain friends with a lot of the people that I skated there with. I think Southbank is an iconic place and holds strong cultural importance. I would argue that it is one of the key places in the UK that people from all over the world purposely travel to try and conquer, and that is hugely important for continuing to inspire and motivate young British skaters.

Candie Bandita (aka Amy Ash), 30, London:

I came across Southbank on a school trip to the (now long gone) Museum of Moving Image when I was about 14 years old. I was intrigued by the dystopian feel of the place and enamoured with the way the architecture was inadvertently a perfect playground for skateboarding. That weekend I went on my own with my skateboard to join in, and it became the place that I would spend the majority of my youth into adulthood. It was an unwanted space, of which we took ownership of and made ours.

I honestly cannot imagine who or what or where I would be without Southbank in my life. I met many people from all different walks of life, encountered so many experiences that I would never have otherwise touched on had I been at skate parks further out of the centre of London. I was exposed to culture and street knowledge, from the highbrow dance, arts and music inside the Southbank Centre, to the drama, trouble and adventure that comes a part of inner-city life. As an adult I am a mural and graffiti artist, and this is a direct consequence of the influence Southbank had on my teenage years.

Southbank is a place where anyone is allowed to be, to share with friends, to be alone, to experience culture outside of your own norm, and all for free. It is a place where people of all ages, classes, tastes and creed, are free to mingle and indiscriminately be among and appreciate each other. It is a melting pot of different inner-city lives and one which does not exist anywhere else in London, or indeed the whole world.

Savannah Keenan, 15, London:

Southbank is a place where I always used to pass when visiting central London with my great grandmother when I was a little kid. We used to stand and watch the skateboarders and she always used to say she would take me there when we next go to London since I had a skateboard, but we never actually ended up going!

However, now I'm older, Southbank is always the meeting point for us when we're skateboarding around the West End. It is the place where I first met the people I skate with today. It will always remain important to me because that's where my love of skateboarding started to grow. I think that Southbank is what gives London personality, and fits perfectly into London itself.

Konstantina Tsapakidou, 32, Mainz, Germany:

I started skating while I was an architecture student at London Southbank University. Living in the area nearby, the Undercroft was my local spot. It was the place where I was going for a break while doing my essays and designs, or studying for the exams, but it was also a place for inspiration due to its location.

Spending my free time skating there gave me the chance to experience a different edge of central London. Due to it I came across the work of Iain Borden, whose book *Skateboarding, Space and the City* was the main literature of one of my uni projects.

Southbank's central location makes people and skaters feel that a central piece of London can belong to them, giving a more 'homely' feeling to the city. It's not that pleasing having to buy a cup of coffee or a meal in order to spend some time by the river.

I am a petite-sized girl, and I generally felt more secure skating when there were few people. One time (it was winter), I went a little bit later than usual and by the time I arrived the last two skaters who were there were about to go. When they saw me coming, they just sat back down and they waited for me to finish my little skate session, since they didn't want to leave me alone. That's the kind of people that hang around Southbank… they truly care about each other.

Camilla Mullins
2012

Camilla Mullins, 23, London:

Southbank has been the one place that I would HAVE to visit every time I came back to London from Italy. There was just no two ways about it. Even if I didn't fancy it my brothers would make me go, saying that if I didn't skate street (and that spot specifically) then I would get nowhere. To a teenager who is extremely competitive that is quite a convincing argument so the Southbank became kind of like my Mecca; not a place I would go to every day but a place I had to visit whenever I would be in the country! Going there still makes my knees a little wobbly from excitement and I've been hitting that spot up for over a decade!

It is always a place you can rely on. If you are feeling down or lonely or whatever you can just go there and have instant mates to chat to and have a good time with! It's a place where young people can go to get away from the so called 'streets', where you can feel supported and part of a community that is there to help you push yourself in new and ever-changing ways.

The Southbank was the first place I ever landed a kickflip to fakie (a trick we all know women love), and it was home to my first ever gap – before that side of it got 'transformed' into a bunch of shops and restaurants of course… Every time I go there it's just a damn good time!

Maria Falbo
2013

Klara Kasparova
2009

Julia Brueckler
2012

Unknown Skateboarder
2013

Lucy Adams, 29, Horsham

I first went to Southbank in 1999, when I first started skating London and we had the *Spots* book by Harry Bastard. We wanted to hit up as many spots as we could on our first day there but we got to Southbank and didn't end up getting to any others that day! We just spent all of our time sessioning the banks. From that first time I went there I've been back time after time and as I've improved over the years I'd think, "'Oh yeah' this is the day I'm gonna do the stairs." It's not quite happened yet though, but it always has the draw.

Southbank is central to the scene as it's one of those last open free spaces. I know there is a rail there now and is almost accepted as a 'skate park', but its always been 'that' place where people flock to. It is a true street spot.

Opposite:
Lucy Adams
2012

Louis Tingle 1986–2004

Louis was my son. He spent the best part of his life at the Southbank skateboarders' Undercroft: perfecting his craft, making friends and participating in the most distinct and diverse space in London, arguably the world. If Louis was here today, I'm sure he would be fighting against the proposed destruction of the Undercroft – in his own way – perhaps sailing through the air on his skateboard, next to the Thames, wearing just a beautiful smile.

Louis was unique, a one-off. Louis's friends tell me of him skating through the Southbank in his boxer-shorts (for a dare), the whole of a sightseeing bus stopping to stare at his 'scandalous skating'. He is not here anymore but his beloved, unique, one-off Southbank still is. However this is not about nostalgia and a shrine to the past – my son will be remembered whatever happens. This is about holding onto something that is alive and well and has great potential to grow into the future. A place where the invisible lines of territorial neighbourhood spaces do not apply, where the snaking lines of tourists mingle with London life and the mutual appreciation of an untamed spectacle is tangibly felt.

The Undercroft is primarily a space made by and for young people where they feel challenged and safe. How many places are there where young people can gather without being moved on? How many spaces are there where there are laughing, carefree young people, inspiring others? In a space they have made for themselves… showcasing talent, fitness and fun. It is as the original Southbank architects loosely intended: leftover spaces to be inhabited and used without being prescriptive and commercial, and it works.

Time moves on and understandably changes and expansions are proposed but the Southbank management believe that 'there is only one way' to achieve this as the banks will only lend if the Undercroft's cash-making potential is realised. And, extraordinarily, people buy into this premise even though there is more than one way to skin a cat.

And how ironic that a 'heritage space' is proposed to document the history of the skateboarders after killing them off! Okay, they are to be moved around the corner to their 'purpose-built' space – an anathema for skateboarders if ever there was one – and maybe they will move on, but to where in this increasingly privatised and theme-parked London?

Let's suspend disbelief if there have to be restaurants build around the spectacle – not in a zoo like way – but perhaps diners could catch glimpses of feet through the air and fast moving shadows. Make the skateboarders part of the experience of being at the Southbank, part of the continuation of history rather than the end of a story pinned on a wall.

The Southbank Undercroft is a true symbol of young energy, diversity, community and Londoners doing it for themselves, so let's not say 'GOODBYE'. As one of Louis' friends said to me after he died 'Louis doesn't say bye. He didn't believe in it.'

Sarah Boyd – Mother, Architect, Londoner
Thank you to Ruby Kvalheim

PAPYRUS
Charity for the prevention of young suicide (under 35)
www.papyrus-uk.org
https://www.facebook.com/PAPYRUSUK

Confidential Young Suicide Prevention Advice
HOPELineUK: 0800 068 41 41
email: pat@papyrus-uk.org
SMS: 07786 209697

Illustration by
Louis Tingle

kung-fu pirate, tiger-boy wanderer, agile artist and skate-boarder extraordinaire...

Lucien Clarke
Frontside Bluntslide
2010

2010—Present

The start of this decade at Southbank has seen skating at the Undercroft go from strength to strength. Now enclosed by a crowd barrier that runs alongside the length of the whole Undercroft, it has become tantamount to a viewing platform for the public and a stage for the skateboarders and other urban artists to practice and perform their arts. The fence was erected to enclose the Undercroft users in the space and to safeguard the audience that gathers to watch them. It has allowed more people than ever the chance to get a look into the Undercroft and to see its thriving community.

The skate scene at Southbank is at an all-time high, with recent tours of the Vans, Huf, Girl, Nike and Adidas teams coming through in the last few years, specifically to skate. Skaters who learned all of their tricks at Southbank are now internationally recognised: Lucien Clarke, Rory Milanes and Chewy Cannon, to name but a few, are professional and well known in the global skate community as representatives of the British scene.

Even though the physical space is now at its smallest, the creative spark of the Undercroft burns brightest, shining like a beacon of originality within an ever more homogenised and sanitised Southbank area. The Undercroft continues to embody the atmos-

Roger Gonzalez
Ollie from flat
2013

DIPSHIT
79TH.

Southbank Skate Style

As the physical and spatial aspects of the Southbank space available to skaters and other users has changed throughout the last decade, so has the style of skating taking place. Many skaters reflect on how those who have used the banks regularly developed a distinctive Southbank skate style, distinguishable from skaters who practised on purpose-built ramps at skate parks. As Lev Tanju remarks, the Southbank regulars are 'are defined in their style and the way they skate'.

Contemporary Southbank skater Chewy Cannon is even more explicit in describing how the space has influenced his skating, he says, 'I skate how I skate because of Southbank, 100%. Thinking about how remarkable Chewy's skate style is,' Joey Pressey claims, 'It's meditation. Anyone who gets to witness that will be inspired and perhaps realise they don't have to be so linear and mundane in their experience.'

Casper Brooker also mentions how important trying new tricks out on the tricky Southbank ledges is for his development, remarking: 'The ledges at Southbank, they're not like other ledges. They're ground down. So you learn a trick in a different way. I always try and learn tricks at Southbank instead of going to a skate park and learning them. Because if you can do a trick on that ledge you can do the same trick on any other ledge...It's a hard place to skate. You've got to really think about the lines you take. It's not just back and forth. It's not just one thing. You've got to figure out how to use the place.'

For Chewy Cannon, the dynamic relationship between the skaters and their adopted space is key to understanding what separates Southbank skaters from those who use skate parks: 'People...just need space to be left alone so they can freely use it, that's what it's all about really. It is a big community that encompasses so many different styles of skating, interests and abilities in so many different areas. That wouldn't happen in a skate park. Skating if you compare it kung fu or martial arts is about that advancement of the style, the pursuit of that vision will always be recognised beyond someone who took a few classes... it's more of a free creative thing.'

Chris Roberts
Crooked Grind

Paul Rodriguez
Nollie Inward Heelflip

The notoriously difficult ledges and architectural obstacles are cited by skaters as part of the process of defining their style. Brooker describes the mental challenge of skating Southbank, 'It makes you think about skating anywhere in a completely different mindset, because you've got to think. Say, if you're doing a trick on the edge of the ledge, like going towards the back wall where everyone stands to get run up for the cheese block. You land and instantly there's a pillar there. So no matter what trick you're doing you've always got to be conscious of what way you've got to go.'

It appears that true Southbank skate style is characterised by a very powerful and spontaneous style of street skating that uses speed, power slides and quick footed moves to manoeuvre over flat ground, banks and any obstacle in your path. It's less of a technical and methodical approach to skating but more about personal expression on the board, it's not about the biggest or best trick but about improving and defining your own style and finding your own lines, which will allow your skateboarding to speak with the Southbank accent too.

Chris Roberts
Frontside Nosegrind
2005

New Talent

Since the beginning of the 2010s, Southbank has embraced an influx of new talented skateboarders such as Chewy Cannon, Casper Brooker, Jin Shimizu, Blondey McCoy, Karim Bhaktaoui and Domas Glatkauskas. These skaters have pushed the boundaries of what was deemed possible and have brought exciting new style and tricks to the Undercroft.

Palace Skateboards pro Chewy Cannon states that 'Casper and Blondey are obviously new generation, they learnt to skate here and you can tell that their skating resembles what this place is like, a street spot and not a skate park. How they use it, is so different to any other youths, you can't go to a skate park and get those kinds of skaters.' Landscape pro Joey Pressey speaks affectionately about Landscape amateur Jin Shimizu and describes how Southbank 'is his natural terrain. Jin's amazing because he just let his style evolve naturally, he didn't go crazy and try and film loads of stuff and break himself. Real natural evolutionary style and you can see that now.'

From the echo filled clickety-clack sounding footage to the squealing powerslides on slabs, tricks by Southbank local skaters have become such an iconic place they can be identified by viewers all over the world by just a few seconds of footage.

Right:
Blondey McCoy
Noseblunt
2013

Opposite:
Casper Brooker and
Blondey McCoy

Chewy's fast and stylish skating style at the Undercroft is well known and has been described as 'natural', 'spontaneous' and 'sporadic' by his team mates and, as Joey Pressey asserts, like a form of 'meditation'. Meditation is a fitting description of the Undercroft and Chewy's skating, and Chewy's new found international fame is due to his skating Southbank where he pushes the boundaries of possibilities to an inconceivable level with each passing day. Chewy says 'I skate the way I skate because of Southbank, 100%," says Chewy, "I've been skating here for ten years solid. If you live in a country for ten years you pick up an accent and that's exactly what's happened to me here.'

Chewy Cannon
2013

Rory Milanes
Backside Tailslide
2012

Opposite:
Rory Milanes
Backside Smith
2012

Kids who I really know, Casper Brooker, I watched him turn from a tiny kid in tights to a full grown man who's super good at skateboarding. You've got Karim, who's grown up there. If he didn't have skateboarding his life would be so different and I'm glad he had an outlet like skateboarding.

Chris Pullman

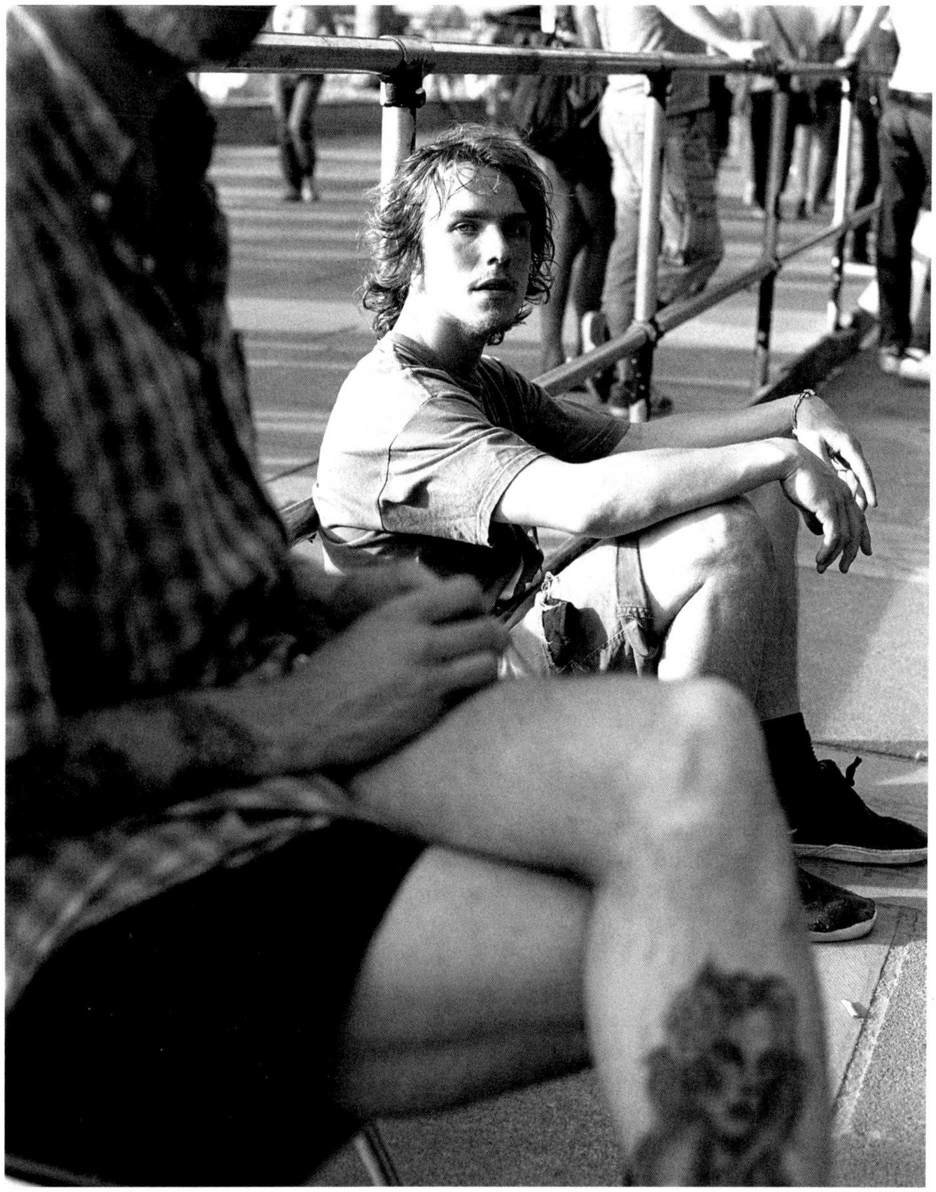

Domas Glatkauskas

Opposite:
Casper Brooker
2013

Chewy's good friend Domas Glatkauskas, talks about his first visit to the Undercroft and the change and impact it had on his life. Domas says because 'My whole view of skateboarding just changed completely. I saw how people skate here and I was looking at skateboarding really seriously, as in yeah I have to skate every day with discipline and I came here and I saw that everything doesn't have to be that tense, it happens anyway but you just have to love what you're doing and you're going to achieve what you want to achieve.'

Jake Sawyer

Skateboarding is fascinating, all encompassing; once submerged the joy is unforgettable, like no other. I don't need to tell you that, you're already reading this. One of the main things about Southbank is that the joy has been lived out there everyday for a long time.

As teenagers visiting Southbank for the first time it was instantly evident that there was a level of skill out there beyond our post-code. We saw the tricks we had learnt, were trying to learn and wished to learn done well, often perfectly, everywhere. There really is something magical about those paving slabs, indeed the whole space, and we were lucky enough to have known each incarnation.

The very nature of our culture encompasses all ages and a room or gathering of friendly faces could often span four generations. Our collective consciousness is alive with memories and apart from video footage and pictures, which document some of what has gone down, this is how it is kept, passed on. We learn from our elders. The generation before me bemoans the railings which blocked off the much-sessioned bank-to-wall, a regular feature of the Wednesday evening skate. Our generation's first great loss was the small banks being boarded off and put out to pasture.

Their disappearance was the first inkling that the threat of redevel-opment – often whispered, discussed – was a real one. Before this, in retrospect, it really was an open wonderland; hallowed ground ingrained in our psyches. When those boards went up an artist's

Mike Manzoori
Backside 50-50

Jason Dill
Frontside Boardslide

collective spearheaded by long time Southbank local Toby Shuall rallied to counteract the loss by adding to what was still there. Blocks appeared overnight. At a time when a good ledge spot was the holy grail this really was a godsend. New life consoled our loss of space.

Our domain was to diminish further. Years later more boards went up to offer storage space for works going on, leaving what we can now see, a third of what was originally skateable. Despite all of this our craft still thrives down there. As a skateboarder I have seen, and continue to see, beautiful and amazing things happen, the solid progression of many people. I have also witnessed a handful of horrible events I will never forget.

Being a skateboarder wasn't always an easy ride. London was different, we were younger, mugging a more commonplace occurrence. Clive Daley, the 'Mayor of Southbank', wrote in an article that the world viewed you as a 'hippy skate bird'. They did: video games championing skateboarding were yet to leak their way in to every home and the X Games wasn't on telly in the pub. In the suburbs, when an evening skate at the weekend met a crew of expensively dressed identikit revellers we were often found literally fighting for acceptance.

It wasn't always the jolly spectacle it is right now, but it takes a while for minds to open – cultures to coexist – and right now we are at an important time in our history. There is no longer that sense of unease down there. Hundreds of people are signing petitions for the spot to stay each day, our views and opinions are entertained in meetings held by the Southbank Centre and after years of adversity from many angles our voices are being heard. This is progress, something which is the very essence of the thing we love.

Skateboarding has evolved, continues to evolve, and at Southbank every change in our surroundings has been met with a different take on how the space is used. Simple things like a rail at the bottom of the stairs, a traffic cone, a board jammed in the drain can change a day. It often takes a keen eye to be a trailblazer in this respect and all of these things are part of our folklore.

Adverse changes have simultaneously caused progression to happen. Bars were placed at the bottom of the little banks: people could no longer skate the banks so they did tricks over them. When bars surrounded the big banks they were skated, hippy-hopped by the Gonz; cut down they were skated a different way; no longer there, the space is opened up and the top of them skated as a lip. Every change, each chink in the spot's armour, adds to every trick done there. When I think back to some of the ledge tricks that went down on the wooden beam it still baffles me.

Locals still find new lines, often opening up a world of opportunities for others. One person's new line can be forever celebrated in the quest for a new accomplishment. In recent years, most notably Nick Jensen, Chewy Cannon and Danny Brady have had a fresh take, and their innovation has pushed the boundaries of what's possible down there. Much of our history, especially the last ten years, has been documented pretty thoroughly, and the internet means that the majority of it is at our fingertips. Now if something out of the ordinary goes down there we will hear about it, but be assured that we will also see the footage pretty soon. When it comes to Southbank, somewhere sessioned so heavily through times when there was rarely a video camera to hand, many of the most amazing things will remain memories, but the tales live on.

Being in one place all day with so much human traffic makes you feel like you magnetise strange occurrences. You certainly encounter people from all walks of life. Here's a story that has never left me. We were skating by the side of the river, it would have been about 1999 by my reckoning, Clive was stood visibly waiting his turn and a Bosnian lady holding a baby walked right into him because she was looking backwards. Clive moved out of the way but she started screaming at him. She wouldn't stop. He held his arms out without saying anything, in a plea for her to calm down and leave him alone. She gave two more shouts, then as he looked away she unleashed one of her breasts and gave it a strong squeeze. Her aim was good: a perfect arc of breast milk travelled a good few feet in his direction and only narrowly missed him. We were shocked. I'm not sure many people have seen breast milk weaponised before. It was as impressive as it was disconcerting. This is just one of the weird and wonderful things that have happened on that river front. I've never had a space where I felt I could share this story but I'm glad it's out there now. Collectively we have many of them, maybe enough to fill another book.

It was a privilege to witness first hand the mythical force that was Tom Penny at the height of his powers. Recently back from a well-documented trip to the States he frequented Southbank. Ask anyone who saw his level of skating then, they will assure you it was mind blowing. One session I remember clearly. Everyone was winding down as night fell, sitting on the beam. Penny started charging at the seven, the only person left skating. Ollie, frontside ollie, backside nollie, frontside nollie. Each trick perfect as always, but landed so much further from the bottom of the stairs than anyone since. He asked someone to call out a trick. 'Switch flip!' I've never seen anyone do a switch flip that fast, let alone down stairs. It's one of the most impressive things I've ever seen. He didn't miss a trick that night. This is one of so many stories just like it. We all have them bouncing around our heads. As much as reminiscing is part of what we all do, I'm glad that tales of what somebody did there still fill my ears on a regular basis. You can feel the history being down there, the river next to you. It's evident the place has a story to tell, a long story with another chapter being written daily.

Southbank – the Undercroft – has a distinct feel to it but also a distinct sound. You can hear the clatter of boards passing any skate park anywhere but you won't hear them a road away. If anyone is skating down there the noise carries. Apparently this echo, something which subconsciously soundtracks our memories, is due to the height of the roof. If it were lower or higher it wouldn't be as far reaching as it is. On a Sunday morning I often cycle across Waterloo Bridge from the south into the City before midday. Each time, just past the Hayward Gallery, I hear that noise: the pop of eager Sunday morning boards. I remember mine being one of them, the first ollie down the stairs in the before-work skate, and i'm glad it still joins them once in a while. When I hear it the memory banks tingle and I feel a sense of pride. I hope I still hear that noise for many years to come.

Winstan Whitter
Ollie

Ben Jobe
Backside Tailslide

Femi Bukunola on Karim Bhaktaoui

Femi Bukunola
2013

Opposite:
Karim Bhaktaoui
2013

Karim Bhaktaoui is an amateur skater for Palace Skateboards, a now hugely popular British skateboarder, he was raised on the notorious Winstanley Estate in south west London and his life and skateboarding have been changed by skateboarding at the Undercroft and exposure to its community and lifestyle.

Karim since he was a 14 year-old kid, life to live, brother of Niheem, always down to do a bid, he'll lift your lid, just because you didn't believe he ever skated all those that hated, back in the day shit, doesn't really matter now he's standing proud, career booming loud, palace wayward boys wearing shrouds, whatever they do, it don't annoy and you're best to avoid them if you ain't down, very seriously now, like two prem teams have to bow, it just the cream and the cows, milk that takes the silk like he skates baby, no place like Southbank to drive you crazy, when the sunny days gets hazy, its all good you can see him by the river, making me shiver as the skateboard delivers, four rolls, or two rolls, or should I say eight bearings and him again with his knees and toes up around his liver, I will give ya, an opportunity to see him skate in this video, soon maybe Lev and the boys will turn him pro, you know how it goes, once you deserve you will always get, Karim baby, nuff respect.

Illustration by
Arran Gregory

Influences on the Self

Through the creative environment and interactions with a diverse range of users of the space, many skaters cite their time spent at Southbank as an integral part of their personal and professional development.

Contemporary Southbank skater Domas Glatkauskas describes the inspiration he draws from the Undercroft for his work as an artist.

'This is my place where I can calm down and not think. I saw all the graffiti and I really like painting and it inspires me a lot for drawings.'

He goes further to analyse how the environment breaks the monotony of mundane routines and creates new inspiration, saying, 'Every day I come down here. I think we're used to routine. Everybody says routine kills your inspiration and you can't have a routine because it will destroy your life. I have a routine. I come here every day but I don't get bored. You don't have to go the other side of the globe to experience something amazing you can come here and talk to a kid and he's going to tell you the best story. Everyone wants to be inspired.'

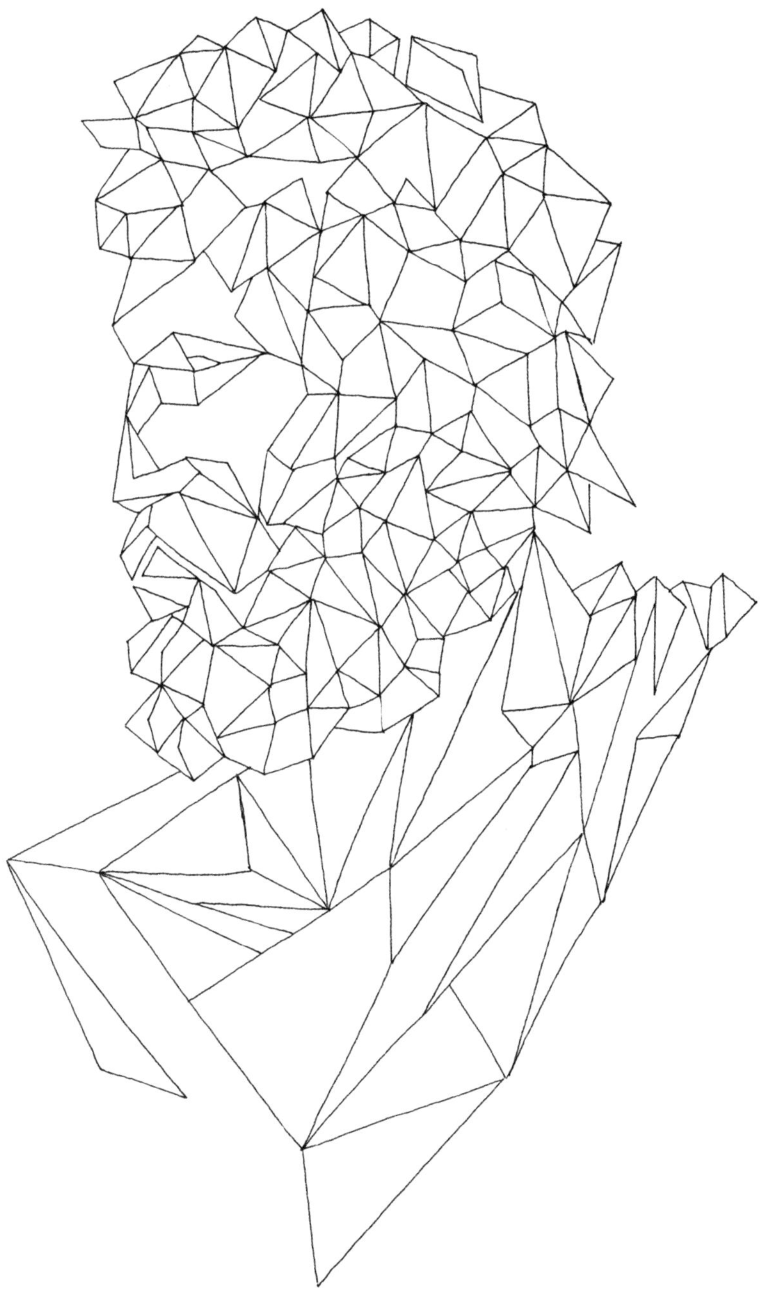

Nick Jensen
2010

Palace pro Chewy Cannon recognises that whether it's the architecture or the people who frequent Southbank, the atmosphere fosters a creativity for skaters outside of the confines of mainstream society. He says, '[Southbank] is the lower ground where you have to start to do whatever you want to do. I think people need that space and he's [Toby Shuall] a good example of what can happen from having a doing space can do instead of being surrounded with a corporate retail space. You don't get any enthusiasm just seeing another generic piece of space, you come here and have a different outlook and you go on to do other things.'

Pro skater Aarto Saari agrees and sees the artistic value in skating Southbank and how this translates into the personalities and lives of the skaters, stating, 'It is more of an art form than a sport. It's a lot more of a cultural thing than just doing tricks and this and that. It's art. That's what bums me out: in a lot of skate parks they kind of take all that away and they kind of mould it into a sport which I don't think it'll ever be. One way or the other skateboarding is going to keep its freedom. Southbank is perfect place to keep that freedom and make that happen.'

Nick Jensen, professional skateboarder and painter, develops this idea in his reflections on how Southbank enabled him to develop his creative practice and has contributed to the artwork he creates;

'Skateboarding has allowed me to let one passion fuel another. Because I get enough money just through skateboarding I can come and buy tubes of paint, I can afford that, and then I can go home and wake up and go skateboarding and that's my job so I'm very very lucky that my job essentially is just like creating. Like I can go and skate or I can go and make a piece of work. I don't have to... I mean I do have another job as well, I'm working as the art director for a new skateboard company, but that's great because that offers a slightly more disciplined side of it and that's come out of skateboarding too. And definitely the style and the attitude at Southbank has informed the style and the aesthetics of the brand. And the things I'm drawn towards in paintings. You can compare the way in which Toby Shaull does a frontside nollie heelflip over a red barrier and lands like that, floppy, to really free, gestural painting. There are connections to that stylistically, I would say.'

Robbie Brockel
180 Backside Heelflip
2014

Beyond the positive influences on artistic creativity cited by many Southbank locals, Karim Bakhtaoui recognises the role Southbank has played in changing his fortunes for the better:

'I come from a rough estate, which is like gangland, skateboarding gave me a separate outlet apart from gang crime to follow something that I wanted to do. I know it sounds cliché or whatever, yeah, yeah, it got you out of the hood but it kinda did. All the people I know like, they all fucking in jail, I didn't want that, I ain't about that, I'd rather be skating, I'd rather be called a grunger by the dudes on the estate, it don't fucking bother me, I don't care. All I know is that through skating and skating at Southbank especially, it's given me a career and not only that, if I didn't have that career I wouldn't have a job at the place where I work, so through the prestige of having a skateboard career I've attained a job for life too, so it's not only kept me out of trouble it's made a whole life for me.'

Jensen also reflects on the way Southbank can influence younger skaters positively and says, 'I think Southbank's key because at such a young age – a developmental stage of one's life. Essentially you're learning that you can be a confident adult at that age and it's definitely made me really look at the world differently. You can even apply it to a skate park still having rules in a more devoid-of-life way – it's a bit like you go and skate, and it's like going to the gym. And that's something that I still feel claustrophobic when I'm around… I much prefer organic – for lack of a better word – spaces. And that's something that I still feel claustrophobic when I'm around… I much prefer organic, for lack of a better word, spaces. And that's encouraged me to think of other cool things to do, creative things to do. And not to question them. And to be confident about them'.

Street Art

Graffiti began to appear at the Undercroft in the late 1980s. Like skateboarding however, it was originally discouraged by the Southbank Centre, who saw it as vandalism. Things began to change in the early 2000s. Following the Moving Units exhibition in 2004, for which street artists were commissioned to decorate the new walls put up in the Undercroft, the Southbank Centre relaxed its stance on graffiti, allowing artists to use the space without the threat of being arrested or moved on. In the last decade, the Undercroft has become one of the most popular graffiti spots in the capital, with artists travelling from around the world to leave their mark on the concrete canvas.

TAKER.HU
12.

95
Since THE 70's
KM8

Artwork by
Seb Toussaint

Mr Shiz

I started my graffiti career in France drawing pieces on paper. I did my first proper wall in Southbank, on the long wall of the skate park. Back then it was mediocre, but with countless hours spent between Southbank and Leake Street practising my craft, I got more technical. I have painted the ceiling with JXC and photorealism paintings at all hours of the day and night. It would be foolish to think something can be done to stop the determination of investors turning the skate park into a retail park, but it will surely be missed. I owe my skills partly to graffiti halls of fame like Southbank. The next kids will have to find another playground to perfect their craft.

CANE MORTO
JAYS CBM
JAYS
INDEPENDENT
SBTRKT-

DUSK
FUTA
SFL

WE WON'T REST IN PEACE
DON'T LET THE SPIRIT OF SOUTHBANK DIE
SOUTH BANK SKATEPARK 1976 – 2013?

RIP OZONE

SAVE SOUTHBANK

SFL
12.

CASPA

JXC
SHIZ

JXC
KROME VISUAL AUDIO
KROMEVA.COM

Fuck Police

13
TOTAL
SUMMER
...MADNESS...

Paul Don Smith

My days at Southbank have been some of my most important as a street artist. The range of people and cultures I have met while painting there has been vast. The vibe of London is right there. It is crucial to have a place like this in this day and age, a place for an urban creatives: skateboarding, blades, BMX, dance, photographic, the list goes on. It all goes on: news features, model shoots, pop promos, film, a great place for audio visual media. I used Southbank to showcase my work, do test sprays of some of my works. A lot of works were born there at Southbank. I especially liked painting the Queen there for the Jubilee, and for the Olympics I painted six gold medallists. The first time I went to Southbank as a child was in 1985 and ever since, it has influenced me. Southbank is a launch pad for the young to explore their confidence and expression; to explore themselves and new skills. It is a crucial London hub for raw new talent to showcase again and again

LONGLIVESOUTHE

ANK.COM
CBM. T17.

Photographers of Southbank

Southbank has influenced the lives, behaviour, and character and travel destinations of many of its locals. Finn Andres and Jamie Rothwell are two Southbank skateboarders who have become photographers inspired by the Undercroft.

Sam Hughes

Finn Andres

All these photos are part of a wider project that I've been doing for the past year and will probably do for another couple of years. I want to make a book eventually about skateboarding in London. There's a lot of skateboard photographers who do very good work, like Sam Ashley and Henry Kingsford, but I don't think in London I've seen a good comprehensive book about the skateboard culture. It's been done quite well in New York by Larry Clark and also Ari Marcopoulos. There's people that have documented the New York scene very well, but I don't feel like any one single person has done a sustained single thing about the whole of London. Obviously Southbank is a part of that but I've got hundreds of pictures from all over London and the Southbank stuff will be a part of a much wider project in the future.

Sam Hughes

Supreme

Arun Grogna

Croydan

Opposite:
Blondey McCoy

Jack Fussey and Tom

Blondey McCoy
Mayday Grind

Opposite:
Jack Fussey

David Yap, Felix Jouanneau
and Jack Fussey

Opposite:
David Yap

Gabriel 'Nugget' Pluckrose

Federico

Jin

Croydan

Jamie Rothwell

You're constantly looking at such interesting architecture, interesting shapes, interesting light, at sunset down here there's nowhere with more interesting or better light than that in London.

It makes you think what you can do with it, how you can play with it, I've got loads of photos of not even skaters but just of people outside and it fascinates me, the range of people that walk past.

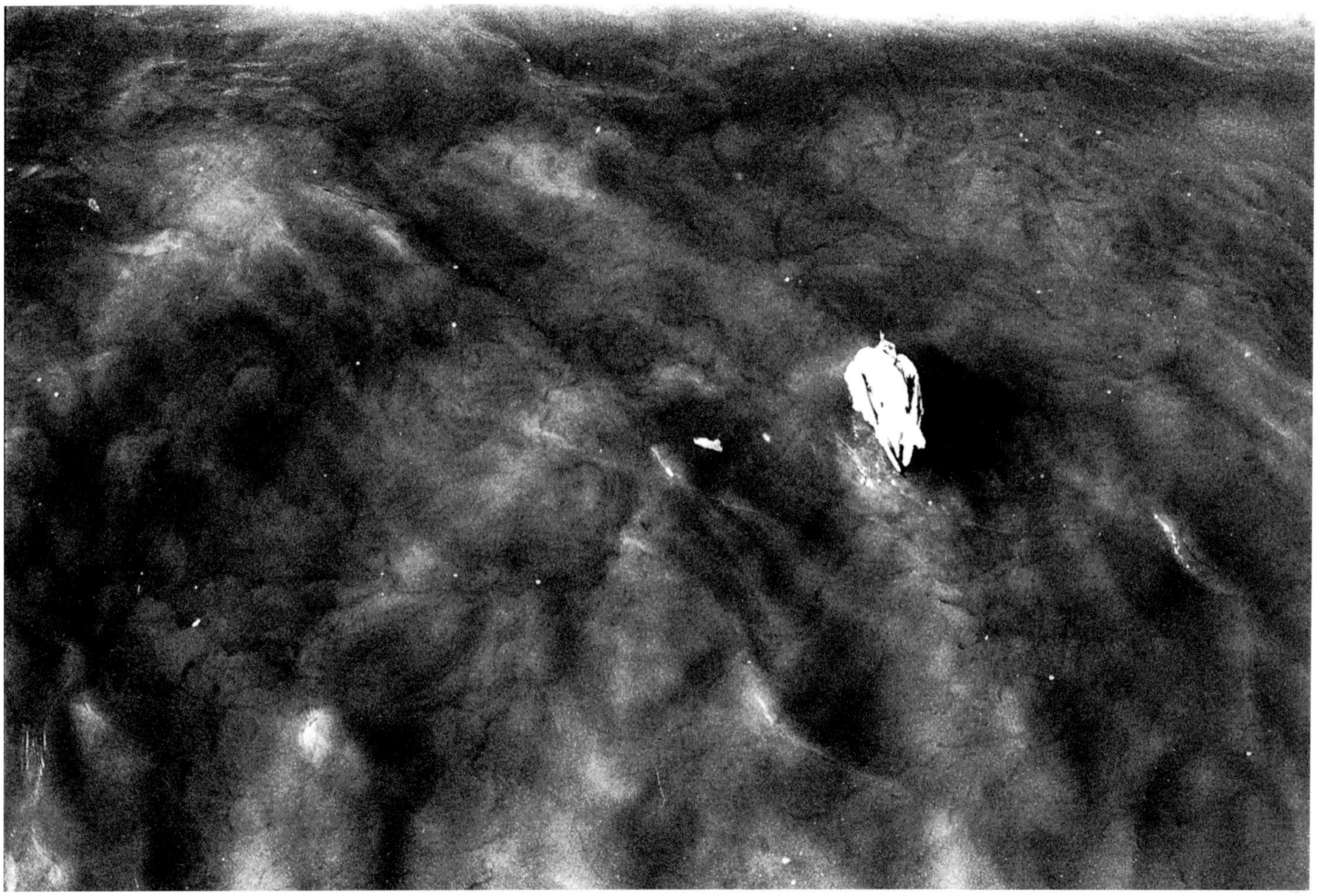

LONG LIVE SOUTHBANK

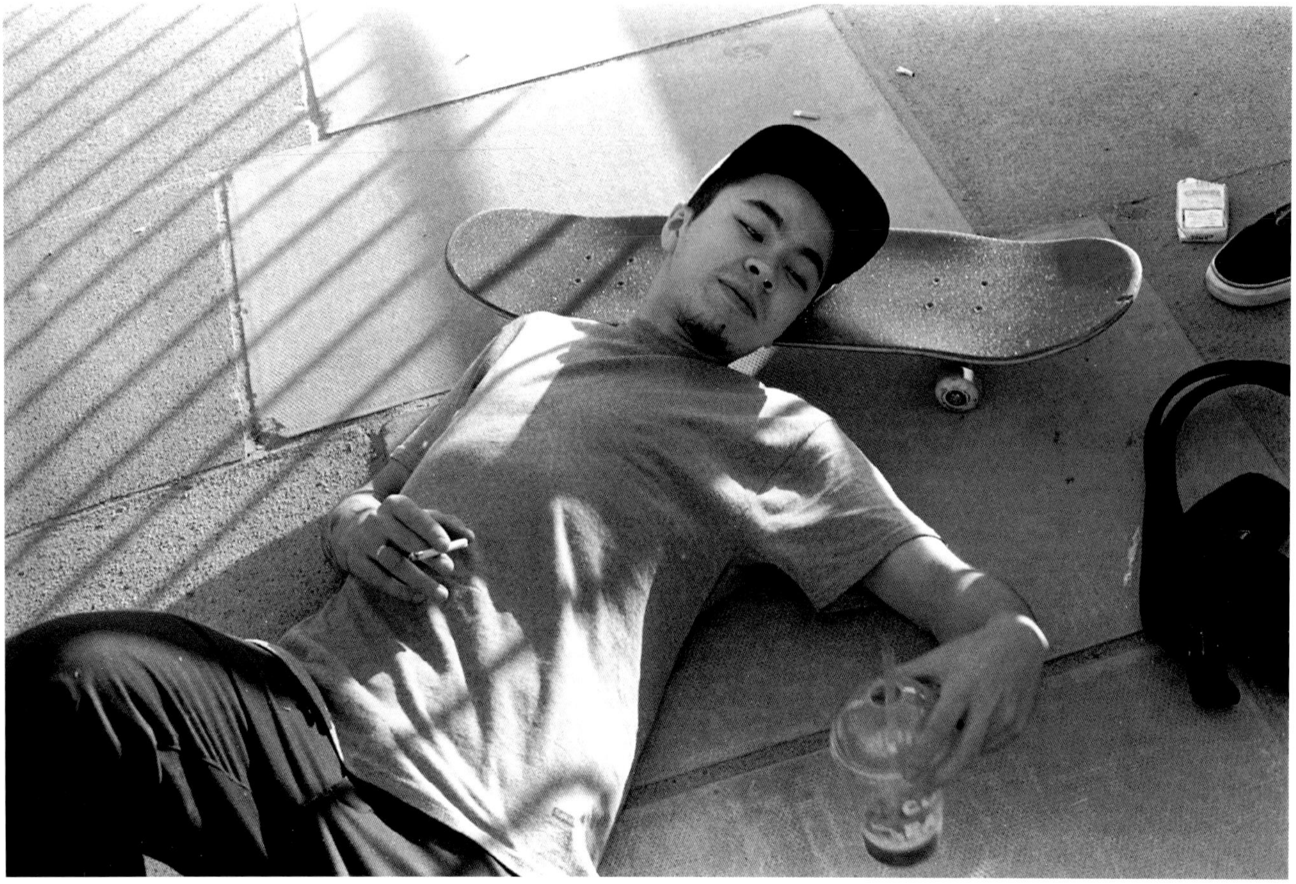

David Yap

DAVE'S
REVENGE!

FOG HORN

Undercroft Illustrators

Over the years, the Undercroft has been inspirational to a number of artists, who have sought to capture its unique essence. In the last year, the Long Live Southbank campaign has further sparked the creativity of the Undercroft community, many of whom have contributed artwork in support.

Tlaloc, God of Rain
Andrew Khosravani

Craig 'Questions' Scott

Zombie

Mellow Banks
Andy Smoke

Jeremy Jones

Nugget & Gnarly Tom
Rob Mathieson

Southbank Comic
Sam Taylor

Lisa Holdcroft

Stephen Smith

Jonny Flips to fakie
Andy Smoke

Trav

Fido Bropho
littleliedown.wordpress.com

Jonny Flips to fakie
littleliedown.wordpress.com

David Z Greene

Mark Foster

Helena Long

LONG
LIVE
SOUTH
BANK

Under Threat Again

In March 2013, it became clear that the Undercroft was under threat once again, as the Southbank Centre unveiled designs for a £120 million redevelopment and extension of the Queen Elizabeth Hall, Purcell Room and Hayward Gallery – the 'Festival Wing' – which included plans to develop the historic skate area into restaurants and retail units.

The plans came as a shock to the Undercroft community, but if the previous three decades of conflict had proved anything, it was that they would not go down with a fight. Almost immediately, an online petition was organised. By June, over 40,000 signatures had been collected, leading the issue to be debated in Parliament.

Angry at the lack of consultation before the plans were announced, at the Southbank Centre's privileging of commerce over culture, and at the threat of relocation to a new purpose-built skate park under Hungerford Bridge, a collective of skateboarders, BMXers, graffiti artists, other creatives, and local residents joined together to found the campaign for conservation of the Undercroft. Uniting under the slogan, 'you can't move history', in April 2013, Long Live Southbank was born.

LAGER
south bank
LONG
LIVE
SOUTH
BANK.

LONG
LIVE
SOUTH
BANK.

Pro skateboarder Arto Saari summed up the objections to relocation, arguing that 'skate parks are one thing, but skate parks don't necessarily breed creativity like places like Southbank do, where it's part of the city, there's people walking around and you're just kind of participating in the community'. Not only would a skate park be a poor replacement for the Undercroft but the spontaneous culture that had developed there, and forty years of history, would be lost.

The group mobilised members of the Undercroft community to run campaign tables at Southbank, initially only at weekends, but soon becoming a daily feature, gathering members for the organisation, collecting objections to the Southbank Centre proposals, and informing the public about the threat to their home. There were numerous awareness-raising events, regular online information films, and countless public interviews in which the campaign spokesperson, Henry Edwards-Wood, and other members of the organisation, compelled the Southbank Centre to recognise the cultural and historical value of the Undercroft.

In addition to the day-to-day interactions with the public – both face-to-face at Southbank and through the media – behind the scenes, LLSB, with the help of lawyer Simon Ricketts, was embracing any possible means by which to secure the Undercroft's future. An application was approved by Lambeth Council for the site to be registered as an Asset of Community Value, securing important recognition of the site's significance to the local community. Continuing to explore legal avenues to preservation, LLSB utilised legislation more usually associated with cricketers and morris dancers than skateboarders and graffiti artists, and applied to register the Undercroft as a Village Green, with protected status under the Commons Act 2006.

The campaign rumbled on through the summer with support pouring in from professional skateboarders, street artists, members of the public, celebrities and politicians. In May, arguably the best-known skateboarder in the world, Tony Hawk, wrote to the Southbank Centre urging them to reconsider their plans, highlighting how the spot has become as iconic a location for skateboarders as Big Ben and London Bridge is to non-skater tourists in London. He wrote, 'I support the Long Live Southbank campaign and its goal to preserve the infamous skate spot. Destroying or even altering the banks would erase an important part of London and UK skateboarding history… I urge you to please preserve the integrity of Southbank, a sanctuary for skateboarders, and an important piece of London history.'

In July, street artist D*Face set up an installation involving skateboarders with spray cans attached to their boards to help raise awareness for the cause. At the time he said, 'It's hard to contextualise this to people that haven't skateboarded, certainly those who haven't grown up skateboarding, but it is to skateboarders the same as the Oval cricket ground is to cricketers or Wimbledon is to lawn tennis players. To destroy this would be a crime and surely the great oak of a building and institution that stands above those humble concrete banks is meant to be a bastion for artistry, creativity and self-expression… Don't let that oak lose its roots.'

BANK

LONGLIVESOUTHBANK
NIKE

When the Southbank Centre submitted its proposals for planning permission in mid-May 2013, LLSB volunteers set about collecting objections from members of the public. As messages of encouragement rolled in, including videos submitted by supporters from around the world, musicians wearing Long Live Southbank t-shirts on stage at Glastonbury, and organisations including English Heritage, the Twentieth Century Society and the National Theatre making public their opposition to the 'Festival Wing' proposals, over 14,000 individual planning objections were collected by campaigners and delivered – by skateboard – to Lambeth Town Hall on the 4th of July 2013.

The same day, Southbank Centre, embarrassed by the level of public support for preservation, made the decision to suspend their application, in order to 'work with our communities to find the best way of balancing everyone's needs'. While the Southbank Centre remained committed to redeveloping the area, said artistic director Jude Kelly, 'we also want our skateboarders, street writers and BMXers to continue to think of this as their home'.

Anyone who believed that the Southbank Centre had learned their lesson, however, or thought that the Undercroft community would now have more of a say, would soon be disappointed. In September, designs were announced – and, in late November, planning permission submitted – for the so-called 'replacement' skate space under Hungerford Bridge. At the same time, the original 'Festival Wing' planning application was resubmitted with no changes to the plans for the Undercroft!

Once again, the community mobilised, this time on an even greater scale than before. Every day, teams of campaigners braved the cold, wet December weather to patrol the Southbank collecting signatures from members of the public opposed to the development, while still more volunteers took to the streets of the Lambeth to spread awareness of the plans among local residents. Through social media, LLSB got the message to supporters around the world that now was the time to take action.

The response was overwhelming. By the time LLSB supporters once again took to their skateboards to travel to Lambeth Town Hall, a total of 27,286 individual objections had been collected, breaking the national record to make the 'Festival Wing' proposals the most unpopular planning application in UK history.

The huge public support for preservation did not go unnoticed, with LLSB receiving coverage not only on national television at home but from news media as far afield as China and the Middle East. Closer to home, Radiohead's Thom Yorke and skateboarding legend Tom Penny were among the many who dropped by the table at the Undercroft to add their names to a membership list that now boasted more than 100,000 signatures.

After months of daily campaigning, awareness-raising and gathering support, it finally seemed as if those in positions of power were beginning to react. Just two weeks after the trip to Lambeth Town Hall, Boris Johnson, the Mayor of London and as such the holder of the final say in determining planning decisions in the

capital, publicly stated his support for preservation. 'The skate park is the epicentre of UK skateboarding and is part of the cultural fabric of London,' the Mayor told a preliminary planning meeting at City Hall, 'This much-loved community space has been used by thousands of young people over the years. It attracts tourists from across the world and undoubtedly adds to the vibrancy of the area – it helps to make London the great city it is.'

After almost a year of ignoring both the Undercroft community and the wider public's overwhelming support for preservation, the Southbank Centre was finally forced to take notice. As calls for preservation continued to mount, the Southbank Centre had no choice but to withdraw their applications for a second time.

Despite the press reporting 'victory' for the skateboarders, the Undercroft community were under no illusions. With the Southbank Centre continuing to threaten closure by the end of the year – regardless of whether or not their redevelopment plans could go ahead – the campaigners knew that the struggle was not over. LLSB's work would continue until the security of the space was permanently guaranteed for future generations. At long last however, it seemed like there was light at the end of the tunnel.

In April 2013, few would have predicted that the enthusiastic but politically inexperienced grouping of mostly young people that formed Long Live Southbank would be able to stand up to one of the largest arts institutions in the world, backed by millions of pounds of government funding, or that a team of dedicated supporters and volunteers would so successfully be able to stall the behemoth that was the 'Festival Wing' plan. One year on, no one can doubt the impact that LLSB has made.

Although it would eventually take high-profile interventions to make the Southbank Centre to sit up and take notice, none of it would have been possible without the tireless work of campaigners or the immense support of the public. One of the outstanding features of the campaign was how it captured the imagination

LONGLIVESOUTHBANK
SAVE SOUTHBANK

‘It is part of the soul of London, that indefinable quality that makes a city a place to live not just exist and work.’

‘Young people have created this space for themselves over decades. It is much loved by Londoners, as well as by tourists, who are delighted by this spontaneous and free expression of youth culture, as an integral part of the more institutional arts centres on the Southbank. It belongs to all of us.’

‘I am a member of the Southbank Centre but don’t agree that we need more commercial space, especially at the loss of the skate park. The proposed replacement is not a realistic alternative, and we need to keep what we have now.’

‘I like to watch the skaters when I walk along the Southbank… it’s art in motion. I find it inspiring and uplifting. We should encourage people to follow their passions and master a skill. It promotes all kind of values that we need in this society.’

‘I lived in London many years before moving to Scotland. On every visit back to London I always go to the Southbank due to it being one of many unique cultural centres in London. The highlight for me is always the skate area where I sit for an hour or so watching people freely expressing themselves and developing their own ability in their art form, whether it be on the BMX or skateboard. I have never skateboarded myself, but by observing the sport you can see it is more than a board with wheels and teenage boys trying to escape – it is a culture, a culture in fact that has a long history that has never lost its following and inspired generations. I would miss this diversity to the Southbank as much as I would miss the book market under the bridge, or, for that matter, the commercially successful enterprises such as the London eye. Southbank is made by the sum of its parts. Take away the diversity of the Southbank and you will kill the charm. Please save the skate area. Embrace this culture, it’s important to the spirit and soul of the Southbank.’

‘Skating in the Undercroft was hugely important to my son and his friends when they travelled to the Southbank from Lewes in east Sussex from the late 1990s onwards – a brilliant example of people creating a real place for themselves in the city, making friendships, animating a dead space, and connecting it with all the other excellent things going on at the Hayward, the NFT, and the NT. It would be tragic to remove this opportunity for young people in future in the name of retail!’

‘The significance of the Undercroft skate area to skateboarders from all over the UK and beyond is tremendous, not to mention the local skateboarders who use the spot practically everyday and keep it thriving. This significance transcends the physical act of skateboarding because of the inherent social aspect, which allows important relationships to form, and in turn helps young people develop their art form in a healthy environment. To overlook the importance of this site is frankly ignorant and its removal would be contradictory to the “artistic” ethos of the Southbank area…’

‘The area is and continues to be a very important part of the global sub culture of skateboarding which helps to breed some of the most creative and talented people in the world and far transcends the sport itself into many other aspects of modern life and art.’

‘As a regular visitor to London, and the Southbank in particular, I always enjoy seeing the Undercroft in use. It is amazing how it has grown to become such a unique part of the Southbank. The way it has grown organically, responding to the needs of the users but without any overall authority in control is an inspiring example of how democracy can work. This will all be lost if it moved to an “official” site and hedged in with bureaucratic restrictions. Please allow it to continue as it is now.’

‘All through the 1970s, 1980s, 1990s and up to the present day this place has created a fantastic, safe, genuine urban community. All have been and are still welcome, no matter what background you come from. I spent many years here as a teen and still visit this area just to be part of this great community. Where else do you get live art, superior talent and a very warm welcome for FREE in London?’

‘This site has an important place in skateboarding’s history. In a time where public spaces in London forbid activities of skating and BMXing, that skate spot is one of the few central places for young people to engage in a free, creative, and healthy activity. It has a positive effect on visitors to the Southbank who watch them.’

‘My husband and I visit the Southbank with the purpose of viewing young people enjoying this particular culturally significant space. It is not a vacant lot ripe for redevelopment but rather part of London’s rich tapestry, which makes it a top tourist destination as well as a fantastically diverse area in which to live. This heritage must not be ignored in planning terms.’

‘I am a 76 year old man and I have no connection with skateboarding. However, I can see that this is a unique and irreplaceable cultural asset, like the Tower of London or Stonehenge. This proposal, which represents nothing short of cultural vandalism, must be stopped.’

‘An organic, raw and human community was formed within the cold, Brutalist forms of the space. This is the essence of the best elements of human nature and should not be destroyed.’

‘As a skateboarder in my early teens back in the late seventies I was aware of the Undercroft as a focal point for the local skateboarding community. Today, as a 51 year-old skateboarder, I am amazed that after the intervening decades, with all the highs and lows of skateboarding popularity, it is still going strong. Please do not underestimate the importance of this organic spot, nor it’s reputation around the world. I personally cannot see the justification for discarding all the years of history tied up in the Undercroft to provide more retail spaces. Skateboarding is still as exhilarating and challenging to me as it was back in the seventies, so please, please ensure that the Undercroft remains the cultural centre of UK skateboarding for decades to come.’

‘If the space was redeveloped into shops it would be a great loss. A space like Southbank is irreplaceable, and although it may not generate that much economic gain, a huge amount of invaluable cultural capital would be lost. There are increasingly less and less spaces in London that are truly free, where you don’t have to pay or consume – a redevelopment of the space into shops would create another of those bland, sanitised spaces that are all too frequent nowadays.’

‘It’s still the heartbeat of London skating and without it it would seriously suffer, there is nowhere else like Southbank and it can’t be re-created. Its been that way for 40 years and i don’t think that will ever change. I’ve spent a good deal of time there over the years and still do and it has influenced my life in so many ways down to what sort of socks I like to wear. My lifelong friends have come from there, job, life and love opportunities have come from there and its the same for anyone who has spent any amount of time there.’

‘Off the top of my head I can think of acclaimed writers, artists, photographers, designers, CEOs of international companies, actors and actresses, producers, cinematographers, directors and so forth that have all spent time here. The Undercroft is as valuable a creative and cultural space as the buildings above it not just as prime real estate!’

‘All I know is that through skating and skating at Southbank especially, its given me a career and not only that, if I didn’t have that career I wouldn’t have a job at the place where I work, so through the prestige of having a skateboard career I’ve attained a job for life too, so its not only kept me out of trouble its made a whole life for me.’

‘Southbank means everything to me, If I thought they were going to close this place down, I’d chain myself up, strap a few big issues to me, stick a load of rocks in me mouth, tell everybody if you destroy it I’ll eat the rocks, swallow them, eat loads of sand, please do not knock this place down it means the world to me.’

‘On Go Skateboarding Day… This year, there were four of us down here; Rob Ashby, Martin Sweeney and Jim Slater. There were two guys filming us, with interviews, as a group and individually. I started talking and I got really choked up and he wasn’t recording, we were just talking and I had to walk away. So that’s what it meant to be me then and that’s what it means to me now. It does mean a lot to me.’

‘The Southbank is a symbol of all that is special about skateboarding, it is a place in the city where you can go at any time without pre-arrangement and meet like minded people to play/practice/socialise/generally have fun. It is still one of the only free places to skate in London that is protected from the elements and is known worldwide as the centre of London skateboard culture. There are so few free spaces in London that allow people to engage in self driven creative expression.’

‘And as far as Japan, Russia, everyone knows where Southbank is. And though it’s not technically the home of British skateboarding, ‘cos there were other places, like Hyde Park … The home of bowl, bank riding and park skating and therefore it has become the iconic home of British skateboarding and long may it always be there. ’

‘Personally I’ve got a lot to be thankful for, meeting the people I’ve met down here, I’ve met friends for life down here, I’ve learnt a lot about life down here – met people from all walks of life. Back then in the 1970s when we first came down, a lot of us were mixing with people we wouldn’t have event dreamt of. Every race under the sun was coming down and you all were one, and there was no bad feelings to anyone, you just all got on because you were skaters, first and foremost.’

‘It’s a cultural starting point for loads of things. Even though it’s dirty and grimy looking, it’s not the best environment in the world, people know it is important for a lot of things and that a lot of things were started there…’

‘It’s a soulful kind of place to be. Cos you don’t have no real set regulation or rules, its just good to have a place to session and just be yourself. Its hard to really be yourself in central London.’

‘I love it. So it would be a shame to see anything happen to it – you can’t replace it, you can’t make it again. It’s a one off.’

‘We came down here as boys and we grew up men down here. It was a safe place to skate and if it rained it was the place everyone came to skate and we became families, a band of brothers you could say. We’ve all got the same interests, we all saw our families grow up, we are all still connected in lots and lots of ways.’

‘Part of the reason London is such a great city is due to it being unique, diverse, energetic and interesting: all of which are encapsulated in the skate park. Not only should this area be protected as a community and cultural space, but it is representative of London at its finest to the wider world: a talented, vibrant, interesting city that does NOT place homogenisation of our centre at the top of its priority list (or one which puts the need for a skinny moccachino over and above the needs of its young people). Plus, as someone who works in the local area, I gain personal pleasure from taking a few minutes at lunchtime to watch the skaters and some of the extraordinarily talented artists in action, and would argue that this is also an important tourist site. It is part of the history and vibrancy of the area and not only provides an important community function and actively demonstrates respect for all different parts of the capital’s demographic mix, but adds an energy and vibrancy to the area that cannot be replaced by another panini/coffee/ burger joint.’

Long Live

Zena Edwards

Clack clack swish
Four wheels score the concrete
With a melody sweet to a youngers ears
Calms his fears
And she's been coming here for years

Clack clack swish
Pound, Dollar, Euro, Yen
There's no currency
Can't substitute a culture, a home, a community
You can't put this song on mute

Clack clack swish
Clack clack swish
A generation shooting the breeze
Metamorphing movement on graffiti slopes
You can't cease evolution by grabbing it by its throat

They're flipping the pyramid on the hierarchy of art
Evolution has its own note
Clack clack swish
Clap clap this
Sing it from the heart
Southbank
Long Live

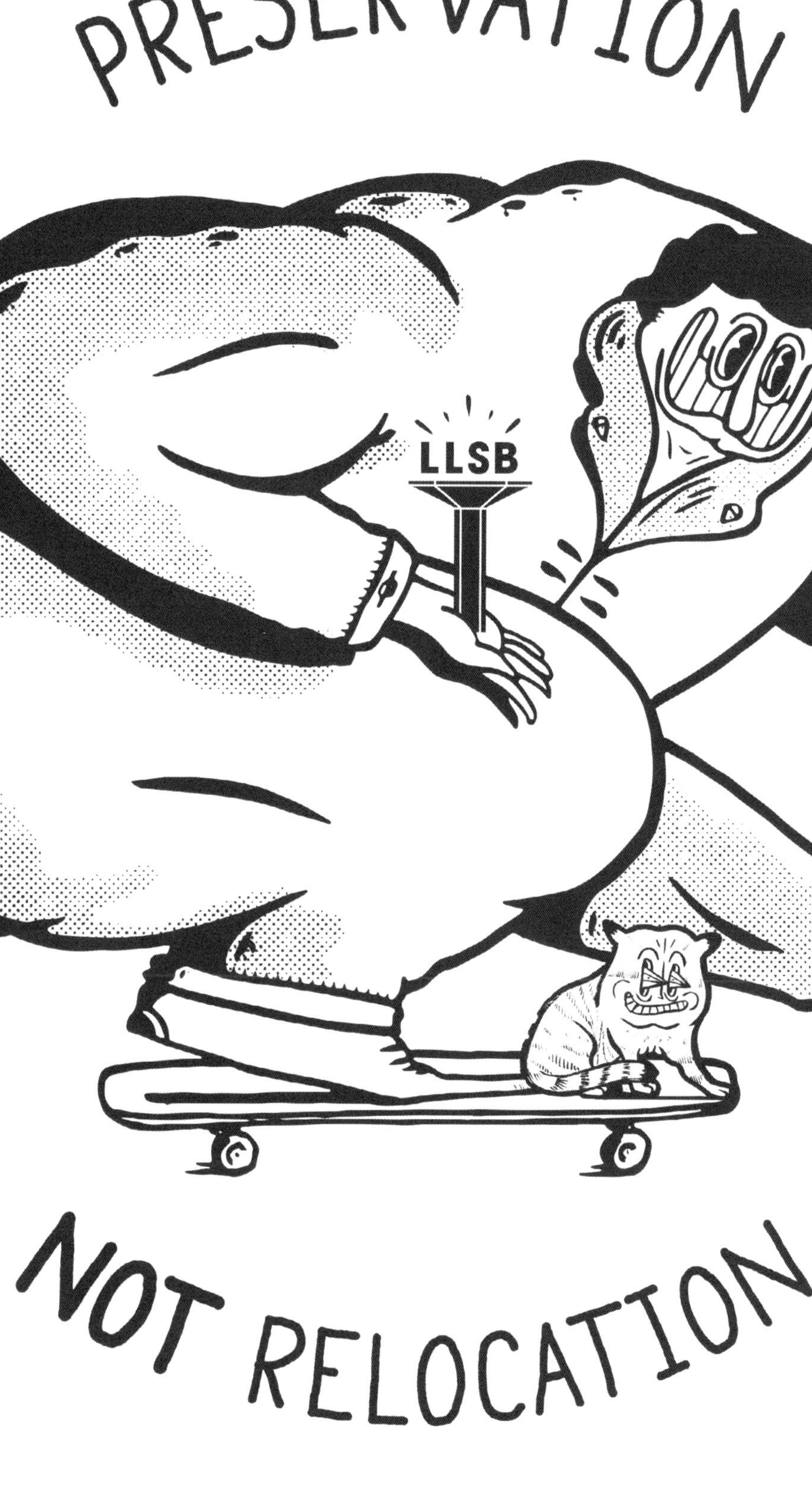

Illustrations by
Darren John

Photography

©Times Newspapers Limited, News Syndication, 1989: 61

Finn Andres: 6, 13, 24, 294–295, 339–347

Rob Ashby: 140–141, 146, 151, 167, 169–171

Sam Ashley: 30, 35, 74–75, 78–79, 84–85, 88–89, 257, 259, 291–293, 306

Sophia Bennett: 382–383

David Binge: 39

Tim Leighton-Boyce: 98, 104, 111–113, 123, 138, 145, 153, 157, 170, 172, 200–201

Mark Boyce: 224–225

Derek Bremner: 36, 40–41, 310, 314–315, 376–377, 379

Edwin Brockman: 147, 156, 159, 170–171, 180–181

Rod Broomfield: 128

Ed Buziak: 101

Elif Chakir: 97

RIBA Library Photographs Collection:

- **Architectural Press Archive:** 42, 68–69, 71, 73, 76, 81, 86
- **John Donat:** 72, 80, 87
- **Daniel Hewitt:** 77, 92
- **Christopher Hope-Fitch:** 65, 93

Stéphane Decool: 102–103, 110, 114–117

Deeli: 231, 235

Ian Dobby: 108–109, 133, 135

Dobie and U-dox Creative Agency: 136, 138–139, 148, 155, 158

James Edson: 256, 291, 302

Chris Eghweree: 96

William Finnigan: 127

Mark Foster: 371

Chris Gascoigne: 308

Brian Gittings: 99, 101, 107, 123–124

Nick Hamilton: 174, 188

Rich Holland: 232–233

Andrew Horsley: 193, 196–197, 210

Alex Irvine: 26, 244, 378–379

Jamie Isbell: 307

Joe_LDNGraffiti.co.uk: 313, 331

Henry Kingsford: 280, 283

Pavel Legonkov: 90–91

London Borough of Lambeth, Archives Department: 44–47, 49, 56–57

London Metropolitan Archives, City of London: 53–55, 57

Magnum Photos:

- **Chris Steele-Perkins:** 162–163, 190–191
- **Peter Marlow:** 161, 164

Dominic Marley: 33, 220, 223, 228, 238, 243

Alec McLeish: 13–14, 16–18, 20, 23

Illustration

Darryl Munroe: 212–215

Ben Norton: 247–255

John Perkins: 124

Skin Phillips: 10

Jay Podesta: 144, 149, 152, 168, 173, 189, 206–207

Cedric Price fonds, Collection Centre Canadien d'Architecture / Canadian Centre for Architecture, Montréal: 59

Richard Rogers Partnership: 63

Jamie Rothwell: 8–9, 12, 15, 22–23, 25, 27–28, 95, 290, 303, 337, 348–357

Fred Schepp: 384–385

Jenna Selby: 268–269, 271, 273–277

Leo Sharp: 82–83, 199, 204–205, 229, 285–287, 289

Andy Simmons: 19, 29, 38, 175, 186, 301

Mike Stride: 135

Seb Toussaint: 312

Andrew Trayt: 118–121

Marc Vallée: 3, 26, 374, 386

Winstan Whitter: 147, 187, 208–209, 226–227

Davie Wilson: 70, 113, 129

Wig Worland: 21, 31, 177, 182–185, 192, 195, 202–203, 211, 216, 218–219, 236–237, 239, 241, 261, 263–264, 266–267, 297–298, 301

Title Page:
Photography by Gorm Ashurst and Tim Leighton-Boyce
Design and art direction by Howie Luke and Rod Broomfield

Sam Boxer: 131

Daniel Clarke: 66

Mark Foster: 371

David Greene: 370

Arran Gregory: 304–305

Lisa Holdcroft: 366

Jon Horner: 94, 178

Darren John: 405

Jeremy Jones: 363

Andrew Khosravani: 359

littleliedown.wordpress.com: 369

Helena Long: 372–373

Rob Mathieson: 258, 364

Craig 'Questions' Scott: 360

Stephen Smith: 366

Andy Smoke: 362, 367

Sam Taylor: 365

Louis Tingle: 279

Trav: 368

Ged Wells: 143

Zombie: 361

Acknowledgements

Long Live Southbank would like to thank the following people for contributing to this book. Without their contributions, it would not have been possible.

Christina Dixon, Jason Caines, William Kraemer, Mike Manzoori, Iain Borden, Paul Price, Paul Richards, Henry Edwards-Wood, Ben Powell, Finn Andres, Rob Ashby, Sam Ashley, Blondey McCoy, Sophia Bennett, Jake Sawyer, Louis Woodhead, Tim Leighton-Boyce, Domas Glatkauskas, Ben Stewart, Max Ellis, Chewy Cannon, Elif Chakir, David Binge, Derek Bremner, Edwin Brockman, Rod Broomfield, Howie Luke, Stéphane Decool, Dobie and U-dox Creative Agency, James Edson, Joe_LDNGraffiti.co.uk, Chris Eghweree, Mark Foster, Chris Gascoigne, Brian Gittings, Nick Hamilton, Andrew Horsley, Alex Irvine, Henry Kingsford, Pavel Legonkov, Dominic Marley, Alec McLeish, Darryl Munroe, Jay Podesta, Jamie Rothwell, Fred Schepp, Jenna Selby, Leo Sharp, Andy Simmons, Mike Stride, Seb Toussaint, Marc Vallée, Winstan Whitter, Dave Wilson, Wig Worland, Sam Boxer, Daniel Clarke, Mark Foster, David Greene, Arran Gregory, Lisa Holdcroft, Jon Horner, Darren John, Jeremy Jones, Andrew Khosravani, Helena Long, Rob Mathieson, Craig 'Questions' Scott, Stephen Smith, Andy Smoke, Sam Taylor, Louis Tingle, Sarah Boyd, Trav, Ged Wells, Zac Leeks, Floyd Reid, Femi Buckunola, Mark Gonzales, Mr Shiz, Ben Jobe, Jim Slater, Paul Don Smith, Mark Slough, Simon Ricketts, Chris Pullman, Lev Tanju, Danny Brady, Emeka Wambu, Frank Nelson, Joey Pressey, Nick Jensen, Robin Lambert, Dan 'Jagger' Ball, Matt Gold, Martin Sweeney, Daniel 'Snowy' Kinloch, Toby Shuall, Louis Woodhead and archivists at the Victoria & Albert Museum, Lambeth Archives, London Metropolitan Archives and the National Archives.

First published 2014 by Long Live Southbank, London, W1F 0LB, United Kingdom.

A catalogue record for this book is available from British Library.

ISBN 978-0-9929268-0-9

Publishing Manager: Ellen Parnavelas
Authors: Steffan Blayney and named contributors
Designers: Andy McGarity and Mark Davis
Researchers: Christina Dixon, William Kraemer and Jason Caines
Printed in Italy by Graphicom